Melissa Murphy is an award-winning freelance journalist and author. She has written widely on health, women's issues and education for national newspapers and women's magazines. She suffered from panic attacks and agoraphobia before finding her own path to recovery. She lives in Bedfordshire with her partner, daughter and black cat.

Overcoming Common Problems Series

Selected titles

A full list of titles is available from Sheldon Press,
36 Causton Street, London SW1P 4ST and on our website at
www.sheldonpress.co.uk

Body Language: What You Need to Know
David Cohen

The Chronic Pain Diet Book
Neville Shone

Coming Off Tranquillizers and Antidepressants
Professor Malcolm Lader

The Complete Carer's Guide
Bridget McCall

The Confidence Book
Gordon Lamont

Coping Successfully with Varicose Veins
Christine Craggs-Hinton

Coping with Age-related Memory Loss
Dr Tom Smith

Coping with Compulsive Eating
Ruth Searle

Coping with Diabetes in Childhood and Adolescence
Dr Philippa Kaye

Coping with Diverticulitis
Peter Cartwright

Coping with Family Stress
Dr Peter Cheevers

Coping with Hearing Loss
Christine Craggs-Hinton

Coping with Radiotherapy
Dr Terry Priestman

Coping with Tinnitus
Christine Craggs-Hinton

The Depression Diet Book
Theresa Cheung

Depression: Healing Emotional Distress
Linda Hurcombe

The Fertility Handbook
Dr Philippa Kaye

Helping Children Cope with Grief
Rosemary Wells

How to Approach Death
Julia Tugendhat

How to Be a Healthy Weight
Philippa Pigache

How to Get the Best from Your Doctor
Dr Tom Smith

How to Make Life Happen
Gladeana McMahon

How to Talk to Your Child
Penny Oates

The IBS Healing Plan
Theresa Cheung

Living with Birthmarks and Blemishes
Gordon Lamont

Living with Eczema
Jill Eckersley

Living with Heart Failure
Susan Elliot-Wright

Living with Schizophrenia
Dr Neel Burton and Dr Phil Davison

Living with a Seriously Ill Child
Dr Jan Aldridge

The Multiple Sclerosis Diet Book
Tessa Buckley

Overcoming Anorexia
Professor J. Hubert Lacey, Christine Craggs-Hinton and Kate Robinson

Overcoming Emotional Abuse
Susan Elliot-Wright

Overcoming Hurt
Dr Windy Dryden

The PMS Handbook
Theresa Cheung

Simplify Your Life
Naomi Saunders

Stress-related Illness
Dr Tim Cantopher

The Thinking Person's Guide to Happiness
Ruth Searle

The Traveller's Good Health Guide
Dr Ted Lankester

Treat Your Own Knees
Jim Johnson

Treating Arthritis – More Drug-Free Ways
Margaret Hills

Overcoming Common Problems

Overcoming Agoraphobia

MELISSA MURPHY

sheldon PRESS

First published in Great Britain in 2008

Sheldon Press
36 Causton Street
London SW1P 4ST

British Library Cataloguing-in-Publication Data
A catalogue record for this book is available from the British Library

ISBN 978–1–84709–030–0

1 3 5 7 9 10 8 6 4 2

Typeset by Fakenham Photosetting Ltd, Fakenham, Norfolk
Printed in Great Britain by Ashford Colour Press

Produced on paper from sustainable forests

Contents

I would like to dedicate this book to all those who helped me through my agoraphobia, especially my mother Carole Murphy, my partner Allan and my daughter Isabella.
I would also like to thank the National Phobics Society and No Panic for their valuable support.

Introduction: A life at home

Agoraphobia is a word commonly used and frequently misunderstood. If you're reading this tucked up in the safety of your home, you'll know that agoraphobia isn't a fear of open spaces or a crowded marketplace. You will know your own unique fears – and they are unique because each of us has different fears and is in a different situation. But it's important to remember you are not alone, that there are others just like you who are too scared to leave their house or step into the supermarket.

I spent a year being housebound. I remember the elation of being able to get to a corner shop and the deflation when on another occasion, I couldn't go further than the garden path. Overcoming agoraphobia is about embracing these highs and lows. There is no miracle cure, no pill you can pop which will dissolve your fears overnight. I would be lying if I said overcoming agoraphobia was easy – it's not. We can't cure agoraphobia because we can't eradicate fear. Human beings have fear built into their DNA – the survival of our species has depended on this reaction. Of course, our survival is not at risk when we step into a busy supermarket. But this caveman instinct remains, and our bodies can't tell the difference between a real survival threat and a situation where we're in no danger.

Each person's experience of agoraphobia is different. You may be able to venture out with your partner or a family member. You may be able to cope with entering small shops or a friend's house but avoid busy places like shopping centres. At the extreme, you may be too scared to leave your bedroom or the confines of your house. Whatever your stage of agoraphobia, one common theme is shared: a need to feel safe. Every agoraphobic has his or her own safety or comfort zone. You may be able to cope perfectly well most of the time inside this zone, but as soon as you try to stretch it, a panic attack sets in. And the longer we stay inside our safety zone, the harder it is to break out of it.

The purpose of this book is to help you redefine this safety zone. My aim is to help you carry your safety zone with you, inside you, so that no matter where you are this sense of safety and calm remains.

People with agoraphobia are by definition isolated from the help they so desperately need. Friends and family are not always sympathetic. They can't understand why you can't just shake these feelings off and get on with your life. They may feel resentful, frustrated that you are dependent on them to go out, irritated that you are not how you used to be – they may even be embarrassed. Those closest to you may reflect a whole range of negative emotions, at a time when you most need their support.

But for many agoraphobics, this support is simply not there. GPs and the NHS are overstretched and there is a postcode lottery as to what advice and help you will receive. Most will offer medication which you may or may not wish to take. Services such as cognitive behavioural therapy (CBT) often have long waiting lists which can be hard to endure when you have high levels of anxiety.

It is this lack of help and resources which has led me to write this book. Inside *Overcoming Agoraphobia* is a comprehensive guide to all the treatments, organizations and resources you may need. During my own recovery, I stumbled across various methods and resources by accident. I often wonder if I would have recovered more quickly had I read a book like this.

There is always a way out of agoraphobia and with the right treatment, many agoraphobics have successfully overcome the condition. Perseverance is needed to overcome agoraphobia – but whether you have been housebound for a month or 20 years, there is a path to recovery. That path may be overgrown with bushes and thorns but it is there, it will always be there. All that is needed is a desire to take the first step. Are you ready?

1

What is agoraphobia?

agoraphobia n. abnormal fear of open spaces or public places. (Greek agora, *market-place)*

This Oxford Dictionary definition probably doesn't capture the true reality of your agoraphobia. It's highly unlikely that you're reading this book because you're afraid of open spaces. It's much more likely that you need help because you're scared of having a panic attack in a public place from which you cannot escape quickly.

Every person's experience of agoraphobia is different, and your own symptoms may change over time. At its most extreme, you may feel unable to leave your bedroom or your house. Or you may be too frightened to go into shops or crowded places but feel mostly relaxed at home. You may feel restricted by a boundary; you may be able to move about within a set area but no further. You may feel calm if you travel with someone but panic if you have to travel alone.

It is very difficult to describe exactly what agoraphobia feels like to someone who has never experienced it. How can you explain that horrible churning feeling in your stomach, the choking sensation in your throat, that sense that you are totally disconnected from everything around you? It can be like living in a bad dream. More than anything you want to get out and about, to do the things you used to be able to. At home, you think about going out and convince yourself that you can do it. You set off, only to return defeated shortly afterwards. It is just too difficult, you could not get through that panic. Something terrible was about to happen, you had to get back home as quickly as possible.

You would do anything to avoid those awful feelings, even if that means a life at home. Despair follows, tears, depression. Why can't you be like everyone else? Other people around you just don't understand. Why can't you pull yourself together and get on with it? They have no idea what that fear feels like, to be confronted by your deepest, innermost fears on a daily basis.

You may feel very alone and isolated but in fact agoraphobia is more common than you might think. The use of the term agoraphobia dates back to 1871, when a German psychiatrist, Karl Otto Westphal, used it to describe the anxiety three of his patients had when walking through streets and squares.

Types of agoraphobia

You may not realize that agoraphobia is actually a recognized medical disorder. The widely used *Diagnostic and Statistical Manual of Mental Disorders*, published by the American Psychiatric Association, lists all the different categories of mental illness and the criteria for diagnosing them. In the 1994 edition (usually referred to as DSM-IV), agoraphobia is categorized as either 'panic disorder with agoraphobia' or 'agoraphobia without history of panic disorder'.

This book mainly deals with panic disorder with agoraphobia as this is far more common than agoraphobia without a history of panic disorder. Generally, people with agoraphobia have experienced panic attacks in public situations, and then start to avoid these situations in order to prevent another panic attack from occurring.

In both categories of agoraphobia, people are afraid of and avoid situations from which escape is difficult or embarrassing. In panic disorder with agoraphobia, the person concerned is frightened that a panic attack will occur when he is in a situation he can escape from quickly. His fear revolves around the symptoms and sensations of a panic attack.

People with agoraphobia who do not have a history of a panic disorder will not be afraid of a full-blown panic attack occurring as they will not have experienced this before. Instead, they will be afraid of panic-like symptoms or something else which could be embarrassing for them, for example, losing bladder control in public. Whatever the case, DSM-IV will only diagnose either 'Panic disorder with agoraphobia' or 'Agoraphobia without history of panic disorder' when another disorder, such as social phobia, doesn't better describe the difficulties.[1]

For some people, just having a name for these awful feelings can be a relief. I remember going through many months of terrifying physical sensations and really believing that I was going insane, before I was told there was a name for this condition and that there were treatments for it. Obviously, it didn't help me get over the condition overnight, but it gave me a name for what I was going through. It also gave me a name to tell other people. I wasn't just being silly, or lazy, or making it up – this was a recognized condition and now I could find out how to overcome it.

I firmly believe that understanding agoraphobia is the key to over-coming it. I would recommend that you find out as much as you can about your condition. The more you can understand agoraphobia, hopefully, the less fear it will hold over you. The rest of this chapter explores what agoraphobia actually is and what may have led you to experience it.

What is a phobia?

Agoraphobia is classed as a phobia, and a phobia is defined as a con-stant, extreme or irrational fear of an animal, object, place or situation that wouldn't normally worry the majority of people. Most people with a phobia will do everything they can to avoid coming into contact with the feared object or situation. Sometimes just the thought of it can be enough to start feelings of anxiety or panic.

Phobias are divided into two types, simple and complex phobias.

- **Simple phobias.** This type of phobia is a fear of a single animal, object, situation or activity. Phobias classified in this category include a fear of spiders, flying, dentists, heights or enclosed spaces (claustrophobia). When confronted with your fear you may react with anything from mild anxiety to extreme panic. Depending on the phobia, your everyday life may not be greatly affected as the cause of fear can usually be easily avoided.
- **Complex phobias.** Agoraphobia is an example of this type of phobia. Complex phobias are a collection of interlinked phobias – unlike simple phobias they are not based around a single object, place or situation. If you have agoraphobia you may fear being alone (mono-phobia), fear being trapped in enclosed spaces (claustrophobia) and fear not being able to escape to a safe place quickly. People with ago-raphobia often find it very difficult to continue with their everyday lives. While spiders can usually be avoided, most everyday situations, such as shopping, working, travelling, even a trip to the hairdresser's, may contain one of the feared situations.

Related anxiety disorders

Generalized anxiety disorder (GAD)

If you have GAD you feel very anxious and agitated all the time. Your anxiety will not be related to any specific trigger and instead of having panic attacks you are likely to feel constantly on edge. GAD is often accompanied by depression.

Panic disorder

A panic disorder is normally diagnosed when you experience panic attacks either frequently or irregularly. These panic attacks seem to come out of the blue and in between attacks you feel perfectly calm. Unlike people with GAD, those with panic disorder feel fine in between panic attacks; they do not feel on edge constantly. A person with panic disorder can go from feeling perfectly calm to experiencing intense panic. As panic attacks produce very real physical symptoms, most sufferers initially believe they have a physical illness. Panic disorder can often lead to agoraphobia when a person starts to avoid public situations in case he or she has a panic attack. More rarely, someone can develop agoraphobia without having a history of panic attacks.

Social phobia

Social phobia is another example of a complex phobia. It is a fear of social situations which can range from public speaking to any social situation such as eating out, the workplace or parties. The phobia is normally centred on a fear of what others think of you, and of embarrassing or humiliating yourself in public. Symptoms of the condition include blushing, shaking, sweating and avoidance of eating in public, using public toilets or other social situations. Many agoraphobics have some elements of social phobia. For example, when you go out you may be worried about what other people are thinking about you, whether they can notice you panicking, whether they will think you are weird. Or you may worry about humiliating or embarrassing yourself in public, and this fear can drive you out of public places when you start to feel anxious.

Obsessive-compulsive disorder (OCD)

This condition has two aspects:

- obsessions – repetitive and unwanted thoughts in response to fears;
- compulsions – acts or rituals which must be carried out in order to relieve the anxiety caused by obsessive thoughts.

One example of an OCD is repetitive hand washing in response to a fear of germs and contamination. Other compulsive behaviours include counting, checking, measuring and repeating actions. It is possible to experience obsessions without the accompanying compulsive actions. Constant fears about germs, illness, death, undesirable sexual thoughts or fear of causing harm to others are all examples of obsessional thoughts.

Depression

Anxiety can be a symptom of depression, particularly post-natal depression. However, suffering from agoraphobia can also lead to the development of depression. Your doctor will try to establish which condition affected you first and which is dominant – the depression or the anxiety. Sometimes a diagnosis of mixed anxiety and depression is given. If you find that your depression started after your agoraphobia it's likely that your agoraphobia is the main condition.

Being agoraphobic for a long time can make you feel cut off from your friends, family and the world around you. You may feel very afraid at times, and if the people closest to you do not understand (and they often don't) this may heighten your loneliness. You may miss the life you used to have and feel that your fears are too strong to conquer. This can all lead to feelings of depression, which makes it even more important that you take steps to get help.

How common is agoraphobia?

There are no clear statistics on how many agoraphobics there are in the UK. This is partly due to the reluctance of sufferers to seek professional help.

Agoraphobia appears to affect more women than men. However, this could be because fewer men seek help. Some research indicates that male agoraphobics are more likely to mask their symptoms with alcohol than seek help.

According to NHS Direct, approximately 5 per cent of adults develop agoraphobia. A survey by the National Phobics Society of its members in 2005–06 found that agoraphobia was the fourth most common phobia among them. In 1987, psychiatrist Isaac Marks carried out a study looking at the incidence of agoraphobia. He estimated that 20 per cent of the population suffers at any one time with some form of agoraphobic avoidance. He also concluded that the incidence of full-blown agoraphobia is between 1.2 and 3.8 per cent, and that it occurs at a similar rate in Asian and African cultures, highlighting that it is not just an urban condition.[2]

Agoraphobia is most likely to start during late adolescence or in one's twenties. It can begin suddenly or slowly and often there is no obvious cause. If no help is received, agoraphobia can continue for many years, often increasing in severity.

Symptoms of agoraphobia

Agoraphobia is usually diagnosed when:

- you experience psychological and physical anxiety when you are in at least two of the following situations: crowds, public places, travelling away from home or travelling alone;
- you are also avoiding the situations you fear.

When an agoraphobic is faced with a feared situation he or she usually experiences feelings of acute anxiety and panic. When four or more of the following symptoms occur, a panic attack has occurred.

Physical symptoms of anxiety

- dry mouth
- rapid heartbeat
- palpitations
- chest pain or tightness
- difficulty in breathing
- breathing too quickly (hyperventilation)
- feelings of choking or suffocation
- sweating
- shaking
- 'jelly' legs
- tingling in hands and feet
- tension headaches
- nausea
- feeling dizzy, light-headed or unsteady
- hot and cold flushes
- abdominal pain
- needing to use the toilet more often than usual.

Psychological symptoms of anxiety

- feeling that you may lose control;
- feeling you will go mad;
- thinking you will collapse or die;
- feeling 'unreal' or detached from the outside world;
- feeling as though things are speeding up;
- worrying that people are observing your anxiety;
- having the urge to run away and escape from the situation;
- feeling on edge and that something terrible is about to happen.

It is possible to suffer from agoraphobia without experiencing panic attacks. If you are successfully avoiding all the situations of which you are afraid, you may experience very little anxiety.

Paul

Paul is 37 years old and has suffered from agoraphobia for the last 11 years.

My agoraphobia started when I was 26 after an episode of depression. The depression I felt made me feel very isolated and I think this might have started my agoraphobia.

A panic attack is like being dangled off a high cliff, not knowing when you are about to fall. It's absolutely horrible. I feel extreme dizziness, extreme palpitations and chest discomfort. During a panic attack I feel breathless and I'm afraid I will go mad or die. I also get tremors. I feel that I have no control over my panic attacks. The only control I have is to stay locked up at home as at least extreme panic doesn't come there.

My agoraphobia started out with me simply avoiding certain situations, like not going to the local shop. I started to cut myself off completely and depression followed. I tried to get out of home but it got harder and harder. My safety zone got smaller and smaller, until my bed was the last zone. I was afraid to get out of bed. I no longer went to social events and lost contact with all my friends.

My agoraphobia fluctuates. I have been housebound for long periods but with the help of my wife I managed to get further and further away from the house. The biggest frustration for me is that I can become agoraphobic at any time for no reason. This leads me to weeks and months of isolation until I claw myself back again.

When I leave my safety boundary, the first thing I notice is that I feel unsteady and dizzy. I start to feel unreal and the volume around me seems to go up. I get flashes of fear and I think that I am going mad or will end up in A & E. My biggest fear is having a heart attack or a stroke. My second biggest fear is being rushed to hospital and being put on heart machines. My third fear is of going mad and never being sane again.

Agoraphobia is my life – it dictates everything. I don't work and most of my friends are gone. I am married but my fear of everything has broken down our relationship and we're having marriage counselling for this. I live about 150 miles from the rest of my family so I can't visit them. I don't like socializing with people as flashes of unreality hit me as I'm talking to them. I've had one holiday in the last few years and that was only managed with high doses of tranquillizers.

Over the years, I have tried about 30 different kinds of antidepressants, anti-anxiety medications and tranquillizers. I have also tried cognitive behavioural therapy, one-to-one solution therapy, group therapy, relaxation therapy and self-help. Out of all of these I found CBT and the anti-anxiety medication most helpful and they got me out the door for a time. My GP referred me to a psychiatrist after trying a lot of different medications. I had to wait two months to see a psychiatrist and a further two years for CBT. Although I found the CBT helpful, once a week for an hour wasn't enough for me. It felt like it was just sealing over the cracks.

My family and friends were initially very supportive but it wore thin after a while. I suppose that people get frustrated when you are afraid of the same things over and over.

My advice to someone diagnosed with agoraphobia is to become well-informed. Get educated about panic attacks and what is happening during a panic attack. Also, make sure you get prompt help for any depression. If I was aware of what was going on when I panicked at an earlier age, I'm sure I would not be the way I am today.

What situations do agoraphobics avoid?

This will vary from person to person, but people with agoraphobia can be afraid of any situation from which they feel they cannot escape quickly if a panic attack should occur. This leads them to avoid that situation completely or only to enter it under certain circumstances, for example if they have a trusted carer with them. You're likely to be very aware of the situations you are scared of, where you have noticed that it is affecting the quality of your everyday life and your relationships.

Examples of situations which can cause a problem are:

- standing in queues;
- large crowded places, such as supermarkets and shopping centres;
- travelling on a tube or train – knowing that escape is not possible until the next station. Travelling on an aeroplane can be another problem although this is also recognized as a separate phobia;
- travelling in a car when someone else is driving – you may feel a loss of control as you cannot stop the car yourself. Or you may feel trapped while driving on busy roads as there is nowhere to pull over;

- eating out – a person with agoraphobia may feel trapped as she knows it is not socially acceptable to walk out during a meal;
- going to the hairdresser's – again a person with agoraphobia knows she cannot leave the salon until the hairdresser is finished;
- sitting in the middle of a row in a theatre or cinema. A person with agoraphobia knows that she cannot slip out unnoticed; she would have to disturb other people causing them possible embarrassment;
- entertaining at home – this can cause panic as it is not socially acceptable to ask your guests to leave;
- crossing a bridge – there is no escape until you have reached the end.

Do you have agoraphobia?

If the examples and description in this chapter are striking a chord with you, it's possible that you have agoraphobia. However, the National Phobics Society has put together a handy DIY guide to assess whether you have agoraphobia. This guide should give you an indication of whether your current difficulties could be agoraphobia. It doesn't replace a GP's diagnosis and when you start to experience panic attacks you should always see your doctor to rule out any physical causes of anxiety.

Self diagnosis for agoraphobia

During the past six months:

Have you regularly avoided situations because you are frightened of having a panic attack?

Have any of the following made you anxious?

- going outside away from your home;
- standing in long queues;
- being in a confined space such as in a tunnel, or on the Underground;
- being at home alone;
- being in wide open spaces, such as a field or a park;
- being in crowded places.

Have you avoided being in any of the above situations?

If you can answer 'yes' to most of these questions, it is likely that you are affected by agoraphobia.

Because agoraphobia is a complex phobia, it can involve a series of interlinked phobias. For example, some people with agoraphobia may have an illness or health phobia which comes out during a panic attack. Others may be afraid to be left on their own (monophobia). Some may be afraid of any situation where they feel trapped, a work meeting for example, showing similarities to claustrophobia. Many agoraphobics worry about what other people think of them or of humiliating themselves in public, which are signs of social phobia. If anxiety is confined only to social situations, social phobia might well be diagnosed rather than agoraphobia.

Panic attacks

Although it is possible to become agoraphobic without ever experiencing a panic attack, most people develop agoraphobia as a result of a panic disorder.

You may have experienced a panic attack in a supermarket, a crowded train or the hairdresser's. The attack may have made you feel so terrified that you thought you were about to die, and afterwards, that you would do anything to avoid feeling like it again. In addition, you may have been worried about what people around you thought of you. Would they think you were 'weird'? You may have thought that everyone noticed you were panicking and felt embarrassed as a result.

In the light of all these emotions, it's no wonder that you feel anxious the next time you go out in a public place. What if the panic attack happens again? How will you get home quickly? What is wrong with you, are you going mad? When another panic attack occurs, you may start to think that it would be easier just to avoid the supermarket and go to a quieter corner shop where you can get in and out more quickly. Or you may decide only to go out with a trusted friend, family member or partner – that way you can return to the car quickly and rely on them to get you home safely. Once the pattern of avoidance starts, it can be difficult to break. Many agoraphobics find themselves housebound, sometimes in extreme cases room-bound. Agoraphobics live in dread of the return of these awful feelings – feelings that no one seems to understand.

Once you start to avoid situations, your normal lifestyle becomes restricted. How badly your lifestyle is affected will depend on the severity of your agoraphobia. You may still be working but avoid situations where you have to speak in public, such as presentations or meetings. You may not be able to go shopping and may avoid social situations such as eating out or parties. Or you may only be able to go out with a trusted carer, upon whom you become very dependent.

Why me?

You have probably already asked yourself this. It is a question that most agoraphobics ask at some time. Why do I have to experience these horrible feelings? Why can't I lead a normal life like everyone else? How have I ended up too scared to leave the house? As explained earlier in this chapter, the fear of experiencing panic attacks often leads to agoraphobia, but it doesn't explain why you started having panic attacks in the first place.

The root cause of agoraphobia and panic attacks is unknown but some experts and studies have shown that the following factors may play a part.

A traumatic event

Sometimes a specific traumatic event can trigger a phobia or panic attacks. If this is the case, you may be able to trace the start of your symptoms back to that specific event. Examples of traumatic events include bereavement, divorce, an accident, or an illness or operation. Repressed feelings can also result in panic attacks. If you have not dealt with emotional feelings and have simply 'swept them under the carpet', they may not disappear. These repressed feelings can cause tension and panic attacks.

Stress and life strains

People with agoraphobia and panic disorder are more likely to have experienced a significant stressful event or period of time before developing the condition. As well as bereavement, illness and divorce examples of stressful events include more everyday occurrences, such as moving house or a new job. Other life strains can include putting your body under pressure by excessive slimming or a poor diet, untreated anaemia, heavy drinking and drug abuse.

Some experts believe that we all have a 'stress threshold' and that there is a level beyond which anyone would panic if it were exceeded. For example, several small stresses may build up, gradually increasing your stress level. A relatively small event or stress can then push you over the threshold, resulting in panic attacks. It is also possible that each person's threshold is different, meaning that some people can deal with more stress than others before reaching the 'panic' level.

Genetic links

Some studies have shown that anxiety disorders are more common among the close relations of people with similar disorders than they are in the general population. Whether this is due to a biological link or the result of conditioning (see below) is not clear. However, up to 25 per cent of first degree relatives of patients with panic disorder will also experience the disorder – five times the rate at which it occurs in the population as a whole.[3]

Childhood conditioning

Conditioning is where a phobia or anxiety disorder develops because it has been learnt, usually from a close family member such as a parent. For example, a mother with claustrophobia may unknowingly pass this fear on to her child.

Personality type

In psychological theories, a personality type known as Type A has been identified. This type of personality is high-achieving, often workaholic, has perfectionist tendencies and is highly competitive and impatient. Some experts believe that this type of personality is more likely to experience a panic disorder.

Oestrogen

Women with panic disorders and agoraphobia often say that their symptoms worsen during their menstrual period when oestrogen is low. During pregnancy, when oestrogen levels are high, many women experience a remission of their symptoms. However, they can worsen after giving birth or during breastfeeding when levels of oestrogen plummet. If you are affected in this way, there is further information in Chapter 11.

Blood sugar

Low levels of blood sugar are a common trigger for panic attacks. Diets high in sugar and unrefined carbohydrates can cause blood sugar to increase and decrease rapidly, causing blood sugar lows. People suffering from anxiety benefit from following a glycaemic index (GI) diet or a protein rich diet. See Chapter 6 for more detailed advice on diet.

Mitral valve prolapse

Studies have shown that there is a link between panic disorders and mitral valve prolapse. A mitral valve prolapse means that the door between the two chambers of the heart does not close properly because the heart valves are too large. Normally, the heart is otherwise perfectly healthy and no treatment is needed. However, the volume of blood in circulation can be lower than normal, causing constant fatigue, palpitations, dizziness and dry eyes. Some studies have indicated that mitral valve prolapse causes both excess adrenalin and excessive sensitivity to adrenalin. Mitral valve prolapse can be diagnosed by an echocardiogram.

Jane

Jane is 54 years old and has had agoraphobia since her early teens.

> I've suffered from agoraphobia on and off since I was about 12 or 13, around puberty. I have had three major episodes of agoraphobia including the current one. But I think I've always had an underlying tendency to anxious thoughts.
>
> My agoraphobia was first diagnosed as school phobia. I remember a fellow pupil experiencing severe epileptic fits next to me in assemblies on several occasions. I think this could have been one of the triggers. The problem escalated from not being able to tolerate assembly to not being able to cope with a classroom situation. I've been told by family members that at a very young age I couldn't complete a bus journey. They would have to take me off the bus and I would continue on foot or get the next bus. This behaviour still persists today.
>
> A second major episode of agoraphobia was triggered by facial shingles when I was about 35. This resulted in a complete inability to leave the house for about a month. It took about a year for me to feel 'my old self' again.
>
> My current episode was I believe triggered by a combination of the menopause, loss of an available car and the way in which my GP dealt with my possible hypertension; she frightened me and did little to support or reassure me.
>
> I don't have panic attacks as such. I become extremely anxious prior to leaving the house, sometimes tearful and shaky. When I am out of the house I feel like a rabbit trapped in headlights, my sight and hearing become distorted and I become irritable. I have never 'run away' although I feel I want to do so. I tend to hyperventilate but only moderately.
>
> I seldom leave the house without my husband or another person; I can manage to get to our local shop a quarter of a mile away and our allotment half a mile away alone, but only with the use of a shopping trolley which I push and an MP3 player.

I can only go on a bus with someone else and then only for about eight stops. I can travel within the town in a taxi, also with another person. The anticipation of leaving my safe area is such that I no longer contemplate leaving it. On really bad days, such as visits to the dentist, my husband will take me in a wheelchair. I can accept going out this way and feel much less anxious. I also have a rheumatic complaint which means I have periods of limited mobility anyway. I have also developed coping mechanisms like shopping online, which have been beneficial, but I feel in a computer-mediated society I am better able to avoid confronting my fears.

I have no real idea what will happen to me when I am outside the house. On transport I fear travel sickness, which has plagued me all my life, but elsewhere I think I have a fear of behaving inappropriately or becoming unwell and causing a nuisance.

As far as treatments go, my first attack in my teens was treated with psychotherapy. The episode in my thirties was treated very effectively with older-type antidepressants (not SSRIs). I am currently self-treating with CBT and relaxation techniques. The antidepressants seemed to be the most effective but did little to tackle the issue of my behaviour patterns.

My current GP grudgingly acknowledges that I have a problem, but is more focused on the physical issues of my health and expects me to find and fund CBT or other therapies myself. My husband is extremely supportive in the sense that I know he will 'look after' me when we are outside and he has no worries about me embarrassing him. He finds it hard to understand how I feel but accepts that this is just part of me.

My advice to another agoraphobic is to be gentle with yourself. Remember you are not agoraphobic all the time, so make the most of what you can do and do not dwell on what is difficult. Refocus your mind on what is really important to do, and let go what is unimportant. I have changed my priorities and no longer make myself ill because of what other people expect of me.

You may have been agoraphobic for so long that you cannot remember living any other way – it is now the norm for you. The journey to recovery may not be an easy one and in order to start it you need to be prepared to stop running away from your fears and begin to face them. This may mean an increase in the levels of anxiety you experience until you have learnt how to remain in the situations you are frightened of without panicking. But no matter how long you have been agoraphobic, one month or ten years, there is always hope and always the possibility of recovering fully.

2

How to get help

When you have agoraphobia, it is very easy to feel isolated and cut off from the rest of the world. This comes at a time when you really need help, support and the comfort of someone with whom to share your anxieties. The good news, though, is that there's a great deal you can do to help yourself and to make sure you get some much needed support.

If you are housebound, the internet can be a real lifeline – although one drawback is that it is now very easy not to leave the house when internet shopping is so readily available! But this will at least enable you to order groceries and other necessary items, and save you from being dependent on someone else to get your shopping.

Traditionally, your GP would be your main source of support. Nowadays there are many other sources – charities, self-help programmes and psychotherapy. Busy GPs do not always have the time or the resources to give you all the information you need. This chapter looks at various ways you can seek help, including advice on work and state benefits, and is backed up with a contact list in the Useful addresses section.

Medical help

Your GP

Your GP should be your first port of call, and can provide access to NHS services and treatments. These are free except the cost of medication – unless you are entitled to free prescriptions. If you are on a low income or are receiving state benefits, you are normally entitled to free prescriptions. See Useful addresses for information on applying for free prescriptions.

The level of support you get from your GP can vary widely. Some people find their GPs very supportive and have no trouble in being referred for other services such as psychotherapy. Other GPs may not be so helpful; they may not understand the severity of your agoraphobia and may expect you to fund any other treatment yourself.

Unfortunately, issues of emotional health are not always treated with the sympathy and respect they deserve. This attitude is definitely becoming less common but you may sometimes still come across it. If you think that your GP's attitude is unhelpful, you are perfectly within your rights to see another doctor. Your surgery may have more than one GP within the practice, so it may be as simple as booking an appointment with another doctor. Or you can change your GP entirely; you can search online at NHS Direct (see Useful addresses). Doctors' attitudes and preferences can vary greatly; some may be firm supporters of complementary medicine while others may not consider these alternatives. So if you are getting nowhere, it is really worth seeking another opinion.

If you are housebound, of course, you may not feel you want to do this as it could mean a longer journey. It can be difficult enough just getting to the doctor's surgery without having to travel any further. But it can be an important step forward to have an understanding GP, and the great majority are very supportive of emotional conditions. This is why if you are facing a negative attitude, it can be worth making special arrangements to see another doctor.

The NHS

The NHS is a very complex organization and not all mental health services are provided by your local GP. It can be helpful to have a general understanding of how the system works so that you know what you may be entitled to and what to ask your doctor for if these services are not automatically offered.

The NHS is funded by the taxpayer and is ultimately accountable to Parliament. With the exception of NHS Foundation Trusts, it is managed by the Department of Health, which in turn is directly accountable to the Secretary of State for Health. The Department of Health's role is to improve the health and well-being of the nation and to modernize the NHS and social care. Next down the ladder are Strategic Health Authorities (SHAs). At the time of writing there are 28 SHAs, and they manage 303 local Primary Care Trusts (PCTs) as well as NHS Trusts. They also make sure national strategies are implemented locally. PCTs are responsible for assessing local health needs and delivering the services needed by their population. This includes specialist mental health services. PCTs deliver primary care services, which comprise GPs, dentists, pharmacists and opticians. Some GP surgeries have a psychotherapist or Community Mental Health Nurse attached to their practice. NHS Trusts provide hospitals, ambulances, special services and mental health care.

When you first see your GP, he or she will assess your condition and see if it can be dealt with within primary care. Ninety per cent of mental health problems, including most anxiety disorders, are dealt with in primary care settings and they make up one-third of GP consultations. However, shortages in psychological services could be one explanation for this high figure.

If your GP doesn't think your agoraphobia can be dealt with in primary care, or if you feel your treatment is not effective, you can be referred for specialized care in a NHS Trust. In some areas, mental health services are provided by a Mental Health and Social Care Trust. These trusts are a partnership between a NHS Trust and a Primary Care Trust. Mental Health and Social Care Trusts may manage a range of services including adult mental health services, care of older people and substance misuse, as well as working with people with learning difficulties and mental health problems. Some primary care services employ mental health specialists such as psychotherapists.

The NHS has to follow guidelines for the treatment of conditions. The National Institute for Health and Clinical Excellence (NICE) is the government body responsible for deciding which drugs and treatments should be available on the NHS. NICE guidelines for panic disorder with agoraphobia recommend psychological therapy, medication and self-help. Studies have shown that the benefits of psychological treatments last the longest.[4]

This means that your GP can offer you medication, but you do not have to take it. Chapter 4 explores how to decide whether medication is suitable for you.

If your GP does not automatically refer you for psychotherapy, you can request it; even if you are taking medication and finding it helpful, you can still request psychotherapy as well. In fact, research indicates that psychotherapy and medication are more effective than medication alone. How quickly you can see a psychotherapist will depend on your area – your GP should be able to tell you this. In some areas, psychotherapy is offered to groups of people with similar conditions. At the time of writing, the government is investing in psychotherapy and trying to increase the number of therapists available to meet the nation's needs. A self-help computerized programme has also been launched (see Chapter 9 for more details).

Private healthcare

If there are long waiting lists for psychotherapy in your area, you may wish to go private. There are several ways of doing this. You can ask your GP to refer you to a private psychologist or you can find one yourself through an accredited organization (see Chapter 9). Many psychologists working in the NHS also see private patients but their availability may still be restricted as they may only see private patients on a part-time basis.

Sometimes private health insurance covers the costs of psychological therapies, depending on the level of cover. However, many policies don't, or apply restrictions. If your agoraphobia was an existing condition, it won't be covered. Occasionally counsellors and psychotherapists offer reduced rates for those on low incomes, so it's worth asking if you are not working or if you are receiving state benefits.

Bibliotherapy

Bibliotherapy is using books or other written materials to treat mild to moderate mental health problems, such as agoraphobia and panic attacks. By reading this book, you are taking part in bibliotherapy! Health professionals are increasingly recognizing the value of appropriate self-help books. Although you may be dubious about the effectiveness of curing a phobia by simply reading a book, NICE guidelines for anxiety and depression state that there is good research evidence to support the effectiveness of self-help. For example, some books use cognitive behavioural therapy techniques and are written by experienced psychologists or psychiatrists. The exercises and methods employed in the books are very similar to those used in face-to-face therapy. Bibliotherapy can be used on its own, to complement medication or as an addition to face-to-face psychotherapy.

Books on prescription

With the shortage of psychotherapists in some areas, the NHS has recognized the benefit of bibliotherapy and has introduced the Books on Prescription scheme to address the shortfall. The scheme was developed in Cardiff in 2003 by Professor Neil Frude, a clinical psychologist. It has proved successful and has spread across many parts of the UK.

Books on Prescription is a partnership between GPs and other primary care services and local libraries. Professor Frude devised an initial list of recommended books and most areas supplement this list with recommendations from local mental health professionals. When you visit your GP, he or she will 'prescribe' a book from this list. You then take this prescription to the library, where you are loaned the book. In the Further Reading section, there is a list of recommended books specifically on overcoming anxiety disorders. Ask your GP if Books on Prescription is available in your area. If it is, you can take advantage of this scheme.

Charities

Charities fill a big gap in mental health services. There are several charities which specialize in anxiety disorders, such as:

- National Phobics Society
- No Panic
- First Steps to Freedom

These charities (see Useful addresses) provide self-help information, newsletters and helplines staffed by people who have experienced anxiety disorders; some provide telephone support groups or offer reduced rates for specific therapies. Perhaps the most important benefit of these charities is that they help you realize that you are not alone. You may have felt 'odd' or 'different' from those around you for some time and being able to identify with other people's experiences can be a great help. Some of these charities run a penpal service where you can write to other people also suffering from agoraphobia.

There are also charities, such as Mind, which deal with mental health issues as a whole. They produce a large range of information booklets, as well as offering helplines and a nationwide network of local support groups.

There is no underestimating the huge help and support a charity can bring. To actually talk to someone, even by phone or email, who really understands how you feel, knows what the terror of a panic attack is like, understands how difficult it is to describe these feelings and what it's like for their family to not understand, is incredibly powerful. You can find yourself finally revealing your deepest fears and worries, at last feeling able to speak honestly. While this may not 'cure' your agoraphobia, it can help you a great deal emotionally, and help to deal with any depression. There are other people going through the same awful fears and anxieties and more importantly, there are people out there who have had agoraphobia and recovered from it.

For all these reasons, it's very worthwhile to join one or more of these charities. They can offer you a real lifeline of support.

Help at work

Holding down a job when you have agoraphobia can be very difficult. If you are housebound, unless you also work from home or are retired, you're probably already unemployed. If your agoraphobia is less severe, you may be able to work but may avoid certain situations such as meetings or the canteen, or you may only travel by car. You may be finding it hard to cope with the demands of working life. If you are at the early stages of agoraphobia, you may be working but finding it an increasing struggle to get through each day.

Your agoraphobia may or may not have been triggered by stresses in your job. However, regardless of the cause your employer has a legal duty to make reasonable adjustments to help you.

Telling your colleagues

Deciding whether or not to tell your work colleagues about your agoraphobia is very difficult. Up until now, you may have gone to great lengths to hide your anxieties. I clearly remember frequent trips to the toilets at work, where I would sit in a cubicle trying to calm myself down. I couldn't bear the thought of anyone seeing me having a panic attack and the toilet was my only refuge apart from my home, which would of course involve a tense and difficult journey back. It's hard to keep this up for ever and there may come a time when you feel you need either to take some sick leave or make changes to your work routine.

Thankfully, employers are becoming more understanding of mental health issues. However, taboos about mental health remain; harassment and bullying sometimes still happen, and your colleagues may simply not understand your problems. If you work for a large organization, it may be worth speaking to your HR officer, who can keep the information confidential and find ways to support you. Some larger organizations also have an occupational health service.

You may simply need some time off, in which case your GP can sign you off from work. However, the cause of sickness will have to be given on the sickness certificate and your manager will be aware of the reason for your absence. At this stage, you may simply be relieved not to have to face the pressures of work for a while. This isn't to say that you shouldn't do all you can to keep working; but you may need some time out to receive treatment.

Making changes at work

You should remember that sickness absence due to mental health problems is just as valid as absence for any other health problem. You may feel embarrassed or be worried about what other people think. The key is to be honest and clear about what changes your employer can make to help you. We are all human. Most people will empathize with your current difficulties and do all they can to support you.

There may be changes you can make to your job to make it more manageable. Are there particularly stressful aspects of your job that could be delegated to colleagues? Could you be excused from meetings if you find this situation difficult? Could you do some work from home or work different hours to avoid busy commuter times? Is there a quiet place you can go at work when you feel very anxious, away from colleagues and clients? These are all issues you could raise with your manager or HR department. If you have been off sick and want to return, can you gradually build up to full-time hours or could your job be changed to a job-share, enabling you to work shorter hours?

Homeworking and distance learning

If you are currently housebound or finding it difficult to move about freely, then you may wish to consider working from home or doing a distance learning course. If you have been unable to work then a distance learning course may be a great way for you to improve your skills, or even to train for a more fulfilling career, while you deal with your agoraphobia. It will also be a good distraction tool, giving you a purpose and something to occupy your mind. When you are unable to leave home, it's easy to feel as if your life has no purpose. This can make you feel even more frustrated and unhappy about your condition. A distance learning course can make you feel that you are doing something constructive with your time.

Courses are available at various levels. The Open University offers degree level courses on a modular basis. For young people with agoraphobia who do not think they can cope with moving away to university, the Open University offers a way to obtain a degree. The fees charged for courses vary greatly but if you are claiming state benefits, then many providers will offer a reduced rate.

If your working life has contributed to your anxiety, then you may wish to consider retraining for a job that is more flexible and less stressful or enables you to work from home. You may be able to negotiate homeworking with your current employer, but if not there are many careers which can be home based, including:

- freelance journalist, proofreader and copyeditor
- graphic designer and website creator
- bookkeeper and accountant
- florist
- ironing service (you would still need to collect and return ironing to customers or have someone who could do this for you)
- pet sitting
- telesales

- life coach
- virtual personal assistant and secretary (virtual PAs carry out administrative duties for businesses remotely, saving the business concerned on work space and costs. Often small businesses, self-employed traders or start-ups use virtual PAs).

In the Useful addresses section, there is a list of organizations that can help you find a distance learning course or homeworking opportunities, or assist you in setting yourself up as a self-employed trader.

The main rule is to balance getting better with not avoiding your fears. Retraining and starting a career based at home in order to avoid ever stepping into an office again will not help you in the long run. Distance learning and homeworking can help a lot while you are in the process of getting better, but regaining your place in the world around you should always be your ultimate aim. If a more flexible career, which enables you to work from home, fits into your future vision of a less stressful life, then that's fine. But it shouldn't be used as a tactic to avoid situations you are frightened of.

Discrimination

As an employee, you have certain rights which mean that your employer cannot discriminate against you or refuse to make reasonable adjustments due to a disability. The Disability Discrimination Act (DDA) places a legal duty on employers to make reasonable adjustments to their premises or practices for employees with disabilities. This includes people with a mental health problem or mental impairment, and agoraphobia certainly qualifies as a disability. You also have a right not to be unfairly dismissed if you have been with an employer for one year or more. The Act requires employers not to treat employees or applicants with disabilities less favourably than other people.

A 'disability' is defined in the DDA as a physical or mental impairment which has a substantial and long-term adverse effect on someone's ability to carry out normal day-to-day activities. This definition includes impairments arising from mental health conditions, of which panic disorder with agoraphobia is a recognized disorder. To gain protection under the DDA, you need to demonstrate that the impairment has lasted at least 12 months or is likely to do so or to be recurrent.

Unfortunately, there are no hard and fast rules about how long it takes to recover from agoraphobia, but your GP should be able to advise you on this. If you are being treated with medication the DDA disregards this and still treats you as 'disabled' for the purposes of the Act.

The DDA also protects against discrimination for past impairments. To qualify for DDA protection your employer should be aware of your disability, which should be disclosed either during the application process or as soon as you are diagnosed.

People with disabilities can be discriminated against in the recruitment process, during employment, if they are selected for redundancy due to their disability or even if their contract is terminated. Employers are deemed to discriminate against a person with a disability if they treat that person less favourably than others and cannot justify such treatment, or if they fail to comply with a duty of reasonable adjustment. Reasonable adjustment may include altering an employee's working hours or allocating some of an employee's duties to another colleague. The employer also has a duty to consider any reasonable request that the employee proposes.

If you feel you have been discriminated against you can take your case to an Employment Tribunal. To get further advice you should speak to your trade union if you have one, or to your local Citizens' Advice Bureau.

Help with money

There are various state benefits that you may be able to claim if you are unable to work due to your agoraphobia.

Disability Living Allowance (DLA)

This allowance can be paid on top of other benefits and can also be paid if you are working. It is tax free and is not affected by any savings or other income you have. To qualify you need to be under 65 and to have had your agoraphobia for at least three months, and it must be likely to last at least another six months. DLA funds a care component and a mobility component. People with agoraphobia are more likely to qualify for the mobility component, which is paid at one of two weekly rates. The lower rate is paid if you are able to walk, but need someone with you to go somewhere unfamiliar. This definition covers agoraphobia because of the disorientation you feel when you are out.

Statutory Sick Pay

This is paid by your employer when you are unable to do your job because of illness. Statutory Sick Pay is the basic minimum your employer must pay. Your employer may have a more generous scheme. It is paid for the first 28 weeks of your sick leave. After 28 weeks, you can claim Incapacity Benefit. You may also be able to claim Income Support on top of your Statutory Sick Pay.

Incapacity Benefit

This benefit is paid when you are unable to work because you are sick and you are not entitled to Statutory Sick Pay. Incapacity Benefit is paid at different rates depending on your age and how long you have been claiming. You normally need to have made a certain level of National Insurance contributions to qualify for this benefit.

Income Support

This can be claimed if you do not work more than 16 hours a week and your partner does not work more than 24. Income Support is paid to people not available for work; for example, lone parents, carers or those who are sick or have a disability and are not entitled to Incapacity Benefit.

Housing Benefit and Council Tax Benefit

If you receive any benefits you may also be entitled to help with your rent. If you pay rent you can claim Housing Benefit and you can also claim Council Tax Benefit, but to claim either your savings must be no more than £16,000. The amount you get depends on your income and other circumstances. If you own a property, Income Support may help with the cost of your mortgage interest payments.

Applying for benefits

Your employer will issue Statutory Sick Pay; you will normally need a medical certificate from your doctor. To apply for Housing Benefit and Council Tax Benefit contact your local council. For all other benefits you need to contact your local benefits office or visit the Jobcentre Plus website to download claim forms or fill them out online. The Jobcentre will be able to advise you which benefit you are eligible to apply for. Sometimes the Jobcentre will ask for its own doctor to examine you. It is a good idea to take someone with you, or if you are housebound to discuss whether they are willing to make a home visit.

If your claim for benefit is refused you can make an appeal. In this instance, it is a good idea to speak to the Citizens' Advice Bureau who can give you free advice. Sometimes wrong decisions are made by a benefits office and can be successfully appealed against. The Citizens' Advice Bureau will have expertise in dealing with appeals and can handle the paperwork on your behalf.

Support from family and friends

Family and close friends can provide valuable support, and having someone close whom you can trust and talk to can be very therapeutic. But care is needed in handling these relationships.

Although awareness of mental health issues is increasing, many people find it hard to understand a condition like agoraphobia. Most people take for granted the freedom to go wherever they like without feeling fear. If you think back to before you suffered from agoraphobia, you may also have found it difficult to comprehend just how much it could affect someone.

For this reason, your loved ones may sometimes struggle to understand how you feel. Those close to you may benefit from reading some information about agoraphobia so they can increase their understanding of the condition. Some charities produce information leaflets specifically for the carers and families of those with anxiety disorders.

A partner or family member we live with may eventually become frustrated and resentful, despite their best intentions. They may want you to return to your old self and may not understand why you can't just 'snap out of it'. Of course, it is rarely that simple, but it can be draining on a loved one to provide additional emotional support as well as possibly doing increased practical duties such as shopping.

Some people with agoraphobia can only venture out when they have a trusted person with them. If that person is also your companion, he or she may feel a pressure at times to be your sole source of support.

There are times when even the most upbeat people have low moods and at these times your loved ones may not have enough emotional energy to give you the help you need. This doesn't mean they don't love you and support you, but it does mean that if, for example, you're having frequent panic attacks, they may find it hard to give you reassurance.

All this can mean that you feel increasingly isolated and that no one understands what you are going through. It can really help if you have additional sources of support – a counsellor, your psychotherapist, an understanding GP or help from a charity. It is still important to talk to your loved ones and be honest with them. But having another avenue of support means you are not solely emotionally dependent on your family and friends. You will also benefit from having independent, unbiased advice or hearing someone else's experiences of agoraphobia.

Summary

- Your GP should be your first port of call. If you are not automatically referred for psychotherapy, you can ask to be, although waiting times can be long and do vary across the country.
- If you do not wish to wait and can afford the fees, paying to see a psychologist or psychotherapist privately can reduce the waiting time. You can also ask your GP about a computerized self-help package.
- Bibliotherapy (reading self-help books) has been proven to be an effective tool for overcoming anxiety disorders.
- Charities fill the gap between what is needed and what is actually provided by the NHS. Many offer helplines run by anxiety sufferers, self-help groups, information booklets and the chance to contact other people with agoraphobia.
- If you are having difficulties at work you can speak to your HR department in confidence. The Disability Discrimination Act means your employer cannot discriminate against you because of your agoraphobia and must consider reasonable adjustments at work that could help you.
- If you are unable to work, make sure you claim all the state benefits you are entitled to.
- Loved ones and friends may not always understand your agoraphobia or be able to give you the support you need all the time. It is helpful to find other sources of support such as a counsellor, psychotherapist, charity helpline or other people with agoraphobia.

3

Understanding your symptoms

You are being held a prisoner in your own home because of one thing – your fears. Or to be more precise, you are afraid of fear itself.

You will probably be more than aware of what your fears are. You will be only too familiar with the terrifying symptoms which can sweep through your body in a minute when you step outside your 'safe zone'. Often these symptoms, such as the trembling feeling in your legs or the choking sensation in your throat, can lead to a full-blown panic attack. And even if they don't, you may feel so tense and anxious and so disconnected from the world around you that it is enough to send you running home. But these symptoms are all signs of fear. So people with agoraphobia are actually afraid of fear itself.

Panic attacks

A panic attack is so terrifying that many people find it hard to believe that nothing is physically wrong with them. You may have been to your doctor several times for reassurance; you may even be worried that your doctor has missed something. In the middle of a panic attack, it is very hard to believe that these feelings are 'just anxiety'. You are completely gripped by the very real physical and mental symptoms of fear. In that moment, it can seem impossible to make yourself calm down and in the end, you are forced to flee to where you feel safe.

After going through this terrifying experience a few times, especially if you also felt embarrassed because it happened in a public place, it seems far easier to simply stay at home or wherever you feel safe. It is incredibly draining to go through intense periods of anxiety. Often when a panic attack has finally passed, you feel very tired. Sometimes just finding enough energy to keep going out and dealing with these anxious feelings can be very difficult.

When you experience your first panic attack, you should always see your GP afterwards. Most people are so scared by the feelings that they turn up at an A & E department or visit their doctor anyway. But it is important to rule out any physical cause of your anxiety. Thyroid conditions and diabetes can cause anxiety, as can certain heart abnormalities such as mitral valve prolapse (see Chapter 1). A physical cause of panic attacks is rare, but it should be ruled out.

Once you have been reassured that there is no physical root to your anxiety, you can begin to think about how you are going to tackle your anxieties. This book will help you tackle your fears in three stages: first, by learning to understand exactly what is happening to your mind and body when you get anxious; second, by looking at your physical body's health and considering lifestyle changes and medication; third, by challenging the way you think, considering psychological therapies and learning to stop avoiding the situations you are afraid of. This chapter explores exactly what is happening to your body when you become anxious. By understanding exactly what each feeling and sensation actually means, you will hopefully lose some of your fear of it.

For some people, understanding what their symptoms mean and realizing there is nothing wrong with them is enough to stop their panic attacks. Most people, though, have to learn how to face the situations of which they are afraid, and how to remain there until they feel calm again. This is a slow process and takes time. In order to begin you need to understand exactly why you feel the way you do. So when you walk down your street and your legs feel like jelly, everything seems to be swaying and you feel as if you are not really there – at least you understand what is causing these feelings.

Fight or flight?

First we need to understand how fear works. Fear is essential to humankind; we would not have survived as a species without it. It's a normal physical reaction to a situation which is dangerous and threatens our survival. Other species of animals have developed their own responses to dealing with danger; for example, hedgehogs hide underneath a mass of sharp spikes and a tortoise retreats into its hard shell.

Humans have been designed to respond to danger by either fighting the enemy or taking flight, in other words running away as fast as we can. This is known as the 'fight or flight' response. This response is triggered automatically and has been fine-tuned during the development of humankind. We also learn to fear as children. We learn that we shouldn't touch fire or step out on to a busy road without looking. So we need fear in order to stay alive. We can't overcome agoraphobia and panic attacks by eliminating fear – instead we need to learn how to manage it.

In order to fight or take flight, your body needs to generate extra energy. It is your body's nervous system which is responsible for generating this extra energy.

The nervous system

The body's nervous system is made up of the brain, the spinal cord and an enormous network of nerve roots which stretch out from the spinal cord. These nerves carry messages to the muscles and organs of the body, instructing them how to react. The body's nervous system works in two ways – there are voluntary actions and involuntary actions. As an example of a voluntary action, we have control over our arms and legs. If we want to get up and walk we can. If we want to open a door, we think about it and then it happens. Involuntary actions are those such as breathing and blinking. We don't have to think about breathing, we can breathe even when we are asleep. Such actions are controlled by the involuntary nervous system; they are not under our conscious control but are vital for our survival.

The 'fight or flight' response is controlled by the involuntary nervous system. To create the extra energy needed, your brain sends messages to your adrenal glands, situated on top of your kidneys, to start releasing stress hormones – mainly adrenalin and cortisol. The release of adrenalin causes a number of changes within your body:

- Heart rate speeds up and blood pressure rises to increase the blood flow and levels of oxygen to your muscles.
- Your breathing gets faster to increase the level of oxygen in the blood.
- Your digestive system slows down as all energy is diverted to the fighting muscles.
- Body fluids are diverted into the bloodstream to increase blood volume.
- Blood near the skin is diverted to the lungs and heart.
- Muscles tense up to get ready for either fighting or running.
- Sweating increases to keep the muscles cool for when they begin to work.
- Our hair stands on end and we get goose bumps. It's believed that this reflex made our ancestors' hair stand on end, making them look bigger – cats also use this technique.
- Involuntary urination or defecation can occur as this system shuts down due to its energy being diverted.

All these responses are designed to give you the energy needed to run away or fight.

Now the problem for agoraphobics is that our bodies are triggering the fight or flight response in the wrong situation. Standing in a long queue in a supermarket is not a life-threatening situation requiring the fight or flight response. However, your body is fooled into thinking it is and triggers its survival mechanism.

If you are experiencing frequent panic attacks, you may be very worried that there is something physically wrong with you. But your body is reacting in exactly the way it should – you need to teach it not to trigger this response in non-threatening situations. This sounds far easier than it actually is. But with a lot of practice, it is possible to retrain your mind and body so that the stress response is only triggered when it is really needed.

The symptoms of agoraphobia can be divided into three groups:

- physical
- psychological
- behavioural

So let's look more closely at each group of symptoms to understand exactly what is happening when you try to leave your place of safety.

Physical symptoms

This group is usually the most noticeable for people with agoraphobia. Physical symptoms can feel very real and extremely alarming. They are triggered by the physiological changes which take place due to the body's fight or flight response. If you have seen your GP and have been told that your symptoms are caused by anxiety, your next step is to try and accept this. This is not always easy to do, and at the back of your mind you may still be thinking that there is something wrong with you. Some of the most common symptoms of physical anxiety are listed below, along with an explanation of how the fight or flight response has caused them.

Dry mouth

Your mouth may feel uncomfortably dry, and you may feel that you cannot swallow properly. This can interfere with eating, so if you are feeling anxious in the middle of a restaurant, for example, it can make eating almost impossible. Difficulty in swallowing can also cause feelings of choking, and you may find that you start to overbreathe as a result. The reason you have a dry mouth is that your body is diverting all your bodily fluids into your bloodstream to raise your blood volume. Increased blood volume is needed to send extra energy to the muscles in your arms and legs and because your heart rate has increased – again to increase the blood flow to the muscles needed to 'fight'.

Rapid heartbeat (palpitations)

A palpitation is a rapid succession of quick heartbeats. You may feel your heart thumping or pounding, or feel every beat pulsating in your body. You may feel as if your heart is going to burst or that it will stop. It is extremely difficult to ignore it or forget about it because you are constantly reminded by its hammering and pounding. Many people with anxiety experience palpitations at night. You may be dropping off to sleep and be woken up by a series of palpitations. Or you may wake up in the middle of the night in a sweat with palpitations. This is particularly upsetting because it appears to happen completely out of the blue. It can also make it very difficult to go back to sleep. You may feel on 'red alert', listening to every sensation of your body, waiting for something terrible to happen in a state of acute anxiety. This is made all the worse by the fact it is late at night, everything is quiet, there is little distraction from your body and the whole world seems peacefully asleep while you lie as tense as a taut elastic band.

When your body triggers the fight or flight response, your heart rate increases to pump extra blood to muscles which need it. No matter how fast you think your heart is beating, it will not stop or give out. During exercise, your heart rate will be equally fast, if not faster, and it is well equipped to cope. Increased heart rate due to anxiety will not damage your heart. Even though the sensation is unpleasant, it's not actually harming you physically in any way.

Constantly quick heart

If you are experiencing a lot of anxiety and find it hard to relax at all, you may feel that your heart is constantly beating quickly. Unfortunately, the more you 'tune in' to your heartbeat or worry about how fast your heart is beating, the more you will feel it pound. It can be very hard to relax, get to sleep or go outside when you are constantly aware of your heartbeat. Occasionally, there can be a physical cause for a constantly quickly beating heart, such as anaemia or an overactive thyroid gland. So you should see your GP and get those causes ruled out.

Once you have been told it is anxiety, it's important to remember that the fight or flight response is triggering the release of stress hormones, which in turn is increasing your heart rate. Your heart is busy pumping extra blood around your body and increasing the amount of oxygen needed for your muscles to be able to fight or flee. Although you may feel that something awful is wrong with you, the reverse is true. Your body is doing exactly what it should be doing. If a constantly quickly beating heart is one of your major or most upsetting symptoms your GP can sometimes prescribe a short course of beta-blockers – these are described in more detail in Chapter 4.

'Missed' heartbeats

Our hearts do not always beat perfectly in time. The heart can often 'skip' beats. In fact, it doesn't actually miss a beat – the beats are in an irregular pattern. So there may be a slightly longer pause, then two quick heartbeats. For an anxious person who is sensitized to the feeling of each heartbeat this 'pause' can feel alarming. You may be worried that your heart will suddenly stop and this can trigger a panic attack.

However, 'missed' heartbeats are perfectly normal and very common in many people. The difference for anxious people is that they are aware of them where most people are not. 'Missed' heartbeats can also be caused by too much caffeine, alcohol, nicotine or indigestion. Again, please remember that they will pass and that they are not a symptom of anything sinister. There is nothing wrong with your heart. The more you listen to and observe your heart the more anxious you will become. It is best to try and distract yourself using any method which works for you, such as reading, watching TV, listening to music or concentrating on breathing in and out slowly.

Feelings of choking or suffocation

This unpleasant sensation is caused by overbreathing (hyperventilation). To increase the level of oxygen in the blood, your body will increase your lung function and rate of breathing. Because your chest muscles become tense it can feel difficult to take a deep breath. This will cause you to panic even more, thinking that you will be unable to breathe. You may 'gasp and gulp' for air, which brings on feelings of choking and suffocation. Because body fluids are being diverted to the bloodstream your mouth will also feel dry, increasing the sensation of suffocation. You may not be aware of these sensations, you may just feel you are struggling for air and be afraid that you will pass out.

If you experience this fear, remember that we do not consciously have to control our breathing. We don't need to remember to breathe, we breathe perfectly well all night long when we are asleep. Despite our overbreathing, gasping and gulping, the body will still ensure that it gets enough oxygen. If you don't believe this, try holding your breath. How long can you hold your breath for? You will find that after about half a minute, your body forces you to take a deep breath. There is a control beyond you. Even though your panic leads you to believe you are suffocating, you can be fully assured that your body will not let that happen.

Chest pain or tightness

Sometimes people with agoraphobia or anxiety experience stabbing pains or tingling in the chest, or just a general tightness. This can be very upsetting and you may be frightened that you are going to have a heart attack. These sensations, like those of choking or suffocation, are caused by overbreathing. When you overbreathe, too much carbon dioxide leaves your body. This causes tingling or stabbing sensations in your chest. It can also cause giddiness (see below), and tingling in your hands and feet. Chest tightness can also be caused by tense chest muscles due to your fast, shallow breathing.

The best way to deal with this symptom is to tackle the over-breathing. Breathe into a paper bag or into tightly cupped hands. Practising the breathing exercise in Chapter 7 will also help. It is important to remember that your body will correct this imbalance of carbon dioxide naturally, despite your attempts to stop it by overbreathing!

Feeling dizzy, light-headed or unsteady

Giddiness is another side-effect of overbreathing. This sensation can be a real stumbling block for someone with agoraphobia. When you try to walk along, everything seems to sway and your vision may be a bit blurred. Dizziness can be caused by certain medical conditions, but that type of giddiness tends to be more severe and everything may seem as if it is spinning. An ear problem, low blood pressure or simply getting up too quickly after bending down can all cause giddiness. However, dizziness caused by anxiety tends to be milder – things seem to sway, and you might feel a little unsteady and feel the need to hold on to something or someone's arm. If you are walking with a trolley or pram you will be holding on for dear life.

Too much carbon dioxide can cause a light-headed feeling. Also, when your muscles are very tense it can affect your body's balancing mechanism. When we are afraid, our eyes dilate to take in more light so we can spot dangers. This can cause our vision to become slightly blurred, enhancing this light-headed sensation.

There is no magic cure for this symptom and it can be one of the most difficult sensations to accept when you have agoraphobia. When you are used to being calm indoors and you feel safe in your home environment, then stepping outside can be an assault on your senses. Everything seems so loud and bright, making you feel shaky and weak. The outside world seems an alien environment, as indeed it is if you spend all your time at home.

This symptom takes time to get over. Practising breathing and relaxation techniques will help, as these will ensure you are not over-breathing. You also need to accept that no matter how weak you feel, you're not going to faint. When we feel anxious, our blood pressure rises; it would need to drop for us to faint. So despite how it feels, when we go outside and feel anxious it is actually almost physically impossible for us to faint!

'Jelly' legs and shakiness

Like giddiness, this is another symptom that can be a big barrier to getting over agoraphobia. When you are outside your safety zone, your legs may feel weak as if you are about to fall over. Some people with agoraphobia rely on props to help them feel steadier, such as pushing a pram, holding a walking stick or gripping their carer's arm. Despite the weakness they feel, most people with agoraphobia at the height of a panic attack can easily, and often do, run home.

Muscle shakiness may be felt in your arms and legs and is equally upsetting. This is simply caused by your muscles being tense for a prolonged time. Try this exercise to demonstrate muscle tension and shakiness: bend your arm, tensing the muscles as hard as you can. Hold on to this tension for as long as you can – after a few seconds or a minute the muscles will start to shake. In addition to tense muscles, 'jelly' legs and shakiness in the legs is caused by the release of adrenalin. Adrenalin dilates the blood vessels in the leg muscles, so that extra blood can be sent to these muscles from the rest of your body. Your body is gearing up to fight or flight and the leg muscles play a vital role in this response. The same response would occur if you received shocking but happy news – for example, if you found out you had won the lottery!

Tension headaches

Tension headaches caused by stress and anxiety often feel like a tight band around your forehead, or as if something heavy is pressing on top of your head. Stress and anxiety can also be a trigger for migraines. Tension headaches may feel different from other headaches – you may not experience a sharp pain so much as a constant dull ache, and painkillers may not always help. In fact, research shows that taking too many painkillers can actually make headaches worse. So it is generally better to deal with the tension in your body rather than rely on tablets. A build-up of tension in the neck muscles and the face is a common cause of headaches and many people without anxiety disorders suffer similar headaches.

Nausea, butterflies in the stomach and frequent desire to use the toilet

Anxiety can often cause a sick feeling or 'butterflies in the stomach'. This is caused by the digestive system slowing down as all available energy gets diverted to 'fighting' muscles. In a life-threatening situation, your body does not need to eat or digest food. This is why that function slows down and why you experience that empty, sick or nervous feeling in your stomach. The same stress hormones that slow down the digestive system also stimulate the colon, speeding up the exit of its contents.

Tiredness

A panic attack or high levels of anxiety cannot go on for ever. There comes a time when the body becomes tired after generating and using so much energy for fight or flight. So you'll probably find that a panic attack is followed by a period of tiredness or exhaustion. This can be a relief to you, but it can be equally upsetting if you feel you have no energy to do the things you used to enjoy. The symptom of tiredness is certainly nothing to worry about. It is a natural response to the excessive energy demands that have been placed on your body.

Sensitization

After experiencing high levels of anxiety or after a trauma or illness, the body's nerves can become 'sensitized'. This means that you become acutely aware of every small sensation in your body. This may provoke more anxiety, triggering even more sensations and leading you to constantly 'scan' your body on the lookout for any change, sensation or new feeling.

If you are troubled with this symptom, again there is no magic cure to switch it off, but trying to accept the sensations and constantly reassuring yourself that there is nothing wrong with you will help. Try not to add more anxiety by worrying about such sensations; no matter how strange they feel, they are not a sign of anything sinister. Learning to relax will help and some people find that they need to learn distraction techniques. It can really help to take your mind off yourself, although when you are so worried it can be hard to do. Experiment with different techniques. Do you have a favourite piece of music or favourite comedy film or TV programme? Anything that distracts your mind from focusing on your body will help.

Psychological symptoms

Considering the physical sensations I have just described, it's no wonder why our mind is so fearful. Along with the physical symptoms of anxiety, we normally have a horrible feeling of dread, as if something awful is about to happen. We can't always explain what this 'awful thing' is, but common psychological symptoms of fear include:

- feeling as if you may lose control or go mad;
- thinking you will collapse or die;
- feeling 'unreal' or detached from the outside world;
- feeling 'keyed up' as your body is on red alert and ready to take action;
- worrying that other people are looking at you and thinking you are mad;
- worrying that you will humiliate or embarrass yourself in public;
- having the urge to run away from the situation.

Some of these psychological symptoms fade away after the panic attack has passed. However, some feelings such as unreality can be harder to shift and are more disturbing to agoraphobics.

Unreality

Feeling 'unreal' means that you do not feel part of the 'real' world – you may feel as if you are living in a dream or are not connected with the world around you. Dr Claire Weekes, the renowned Australian pioneer in panic disorder, describes it as a 'narrowing of interest that leads to a feeling of withdrawal from the outside world, as if there is a veil between it and him [the person with agoraphobia], a veil he can neither lift aside nor break through'.

Unreality, or depersonalization as it is sometimes called, is normally caused by you paying less attention to the outside world and more attention to yourself. If you are housebound and spend most of your time on 'red alert' looking out for a new, 'dangerous' bodily symptom it is easy to lose interest in the world around you. Because you are so afraid of your symptoms, everything else seems less important.

But even if you didn't have agoraphobia, if you hadn't left the house for a few weeks it would feel strange when you first went outside again. The difference is that someone without agoraphobia wouldn't be afraid of this strangeness and would carry on. For people with agoraphobia, this disconnection from their surroundings is another trigger of anxiety. If unreality is one of your symptoms, be assured that this is not a sign that you are getting worse, going mad or developing another psychological disorder. It is a perfectly natural reaction given your circumstances. The best way to deal with it is to accept it for now and try not to give it any extra attention. As you start to deal with your anxiety, this symptom will fade. Dealing with your thoughts and psychological symptoms is covered in detail in Chapter 8.

Behavioural symptoms

The combined physical and psychological symptoms of anxiety can lead to behavioural symptoms. This means we change our behaviour because of our physical and psychological symptoms.

Avoidance

The most common behavioural symptom of agoraphobia, and of many other phobias, is avoidance. For example, if we have a panic attack in a supermarket we may then avoid going into the supermarket again in case another panic attack happens. If we feel calm at home and anxious when we leave, then it seems easier to avoid going out. It's only natural that we would do anything to stop the terrifying symptoms of a panic attack from returning.

Other examples of avoidance include:

- avoiding public transport and only travelling by car;
- only going out anywhere when you are with a trusted friend or family member;
- driving on quiet roads, not dual carriageways or motorways;
- only shopping at quiet times, for example at night;
- wearing sunglasses whenever you go out or only going out when you are pushing a pram;
- always sitting near to the exit at cinemas, theatres or restaurants.

Unfortunately, once we start avoiding situations, we are only reinforcing our fears. Our behaviour is confirming that the psychological and physical symptoms are the correct response to the perceived 'danger'. The secret of overcoming agoraphobia is to change our behaviour, for example to stop avoiding situations and learn how to remain in any situation until the feelings of panic subside.

It may seem as if your panic attacks happen out of the blue. Or you may think that simply leaving a situation in which you feel comfortable is what triggers your anxiety. However, as we will see in Chapter 8, there are specific triggers which can set off the spiral of anxiety. Understanding these triggers is the key to taking control of your anxiety. But in order to do this it is a good idea to prepare yourself by ensuring you are taking any medication you need, learning some relaxation techniques and making sure that your lifestyle is not a barrier to you getting better. The next few chapters show you how to do this.

4

Medication

The question of whether to take medication or not can be a very difficult one for people with agoraphobia. You may feel anxious at the thought of taking medication, you may not think it will help you, or you may be worried about becoming dependent on it. However, medication can have a positive role to play in overcoming agoraphobia and acute anxiety. It is believed to be most effective when combined with cognitive behavioural therapy. Many people with anxiety have found relief through medication from some of the physical and emotional symptoms, giving them a 'kick-start' to tackle their agoraphobia.

As we saw in Chapter 2, the National Institute for Health and Clinical Excellence (NICE) decides which drugs and treatments should be available on the NHS. The most common medications prescribed to people with agoraphobia are antidepressants, of which there are six types. Beta-blockers are sometimes also prescribed for a short period for acute anxiety symptoms such as agitation or palpitations.

When considering whether to take medication you should discuss the following with your GP:

- how the medicine works;
- any long-term risks of taking the medicine;
- possible interactions with any other medicines you are taking;
- any potential side-effects and what you would be comfortable with;
- whether you are pregnant, breastfeeding or planning a family.

Your GP should also provide you with written information or a fact sheet about the medication.

Antidepressants

Despite the name, antidepressants are not just used to treat depression. They are also used to treat conditions such as panic disorder, obsessive-compulsive disorders and bulimia.

Out of the six types of antidepressants, NICE guidelines recommend the Selective Serotonin Reuptake Inhibitors (SSRIs) group for

agoraphobia. There are many different types of SSRIs, including citalo-
pram, escitalopram, fluoxetine, paroxetine and sertraline. All of these
are available under different brand names. If one type doesn't suit you
this doesn't mean that none of them will. Changing to a different SSRI
or altering the dose can be worthwhile. If you find that SSRIs are not
suitable for you, imipramine or clomipramine may be offered. These
belong to the group known as 'tricyclic antidepressants'. You should
not normally be prescribed medicines of the types known as antipsy-
chotics or sedative antihistamines, or benzodiazepines (tranquillizers),
for agoraphobia.

Antidepressants work by altering the balance of chemicals in the
brain called neurotransmitters. Neurotransmitters are what enable
nerve cells or neurons in the brain to communicate with each other.
Neurotransmitters are released by one neuron and interact with the
receptors on another neuron. Their action is terminated by being taken
back up into the neuron that released them. This is called reuptake.

Depression and other conditions such as panic disorder are thought
to be associated with low levels of certain neurotransmitters, particularly serotonin and noradrenalin. SSRI antidepressants work by
increasing the levels of serotonin and prolonging its effect. This is
done by blocking the neuron's reuptake of serotonin. Tricyclic antidepressants work by blocking the reuptake of both noradrenalin and
serotonin but are associated with greater side-effects than SSRIs. A
newer type of antidepressant called venlafaxine has been licensed for
generalized anxiety disorder. This works in a very similar way to SSRIs
and blocks the reuptake of serotonin and noradrenalin at higher doses.
It has fewer side-effects than tricyclic antidepressants.

Starting antidepressants

People can sometimes feel guilty or even ashamed of taking antidepressants. Although the subject may be taboo, you would probably be
surprised at how many people have used them. In 2005, 27.7 million
antidepressants were prescribed in England.[5] So it's quite likely that you
already know someone who has used them. You wouldn't feel ashamed
or uneasy about taking medication for diabetes, asthma or a broken leg.
Why feel differently about treating any other condition?

You will need to see your GP regularly when first starting an antidepressant and then at regular intervals to monitor if the medication is
helping you. If you find the antidepressant is helping you, it is usual
to stay on the treatment for at least six months after you start to feel
better. A longer course may be needed if you have been agoraphobic

for a long time or have had recurrent episodes. It is important to take the medication for the prescribed length of time, as research has shown that if you stop an antidepressant too quickly, your original symptoms may rapidly return.

Alcohol can interfere with medication in various ways; it can increase or decrease its action. You should ask your GP whether you can drink alcohol, as this may vary according to the type of medication taken.

It is normal to experience heightened levels of anxiety when first taking an antidepressant, and this anxiety can last for several weeks. You may be worried about possible side-effects, while mild side-effects from the medication itself can result in increased anxiety. When you have spent so long worrying about what your physical symptoms mean, it is only natural to worry about the start of any new physical sensation. However, most side-effects of antidepressants are mild and tend to wear off after a couple of weeks. Some of the most common side-effects are a dry mouth, nausea, headaches, diarrhoea, and sexual difficulty such as loss of sex drive or inability to ejaculate. Not everyone experiences side-effects on antidepressants. If you don't experience any, this doesn't mean the medication is not working.

During the first few days of taking an antidepressant, it is a good idea to practise your relaxation techniques more frequently than usual. This is not the time to challenge yourself, so avoid situations which provoke your anxiety until you feel comfortable on your medication, and you feel in a position gradually to start to face such situations.

Antidepressants do not work immediately. It is normally between two and four weeks before they start taking effect. However, it can be a few months before you start to 'feel' different and notice any improvement. It is important to keep taking your antidepressant during this time even if you think it is having no effect. You should not stop your medication suddenly without seeing your GP first.

Side-effects

By law, a pharmaceutical company has to list every possible side-effect that could occur. This can make very uneasy reading for someone who suffers from panic attacks, so please do not dwell on it! However, it is important to remember that people who do experience side-effects find that they are mild and soon wear off. If you experience a side-effect that you cannot bear and is making you feel ill or too anxious, go back to your GP. SSRIs vary and it is worthwhile trying more than one if the first choice is not effective. You may find that another one causes no side-effects.

Another option is to start on a low dose and gradually increase it. This will minimize the possibility of any side-effects.

Some people experience heartburn or other digestive problems when taking medication. This can be avoided by taking your tablet after a meal. Getting into this routine should also help you remember to take it each day. It is a good idea to take the tablet around the same time each day, for example after dinner. This will maintain even levels of the medication in your body.

Are antidepressants dangerous or addictive?

There has been some media coverage of the increased risk of suicide in patients taking antidepressants for depression. In 2004, the then Committee on Safety of Medicines (CSM) reviewed the evidence on whether there was a link between SSRI antidepressants and suicide and could find no evidence to support it.[6]

There has also been negative media coverage about withdrawal effects from antidepressants. Antidepressants are not classed as an addictive drug – you do not need to take an increasing amount of the drug to have the same effect and to avoid unpleasant withdrawal symptoms. However, antidepressants can cause unpleasant symptoms called 'discontinuation symptoms' – also sometimes referred to as 'withdrawal symptoms' – when you stop taking them, or when you miss doses or reduce the dose. These symptoms can include dizziness, numbness and tingling, nausea and vomiting, headache, sweating, anxiety and sleep disturbances.

Usually any discontinuation symptoms are mild, but they can be severe if the antidepressant is stopped abruptly. When the time comes for you to stop taking antidepressants, you will normally gradually decrease the dose to avoid any possible withdrawal symptoms.

Beta-blockers

If you are suffering from acute anxiety as well as agoraphobia, your GP may prescribe a short course of beta-blockers. These are used to reduce the physical symptoms of anxiety, such as palpitations or agitation. They work by slowing the heart rate and reducing blood pressure. The drug most commonly used for anxiety is propranolol (brand name Inderal). Tranquillizers are well known for causing dependency and withdrawal symptoms so they are rarely used for anxiety. They are only used in the short term for the severest cases of anxiety, rarely for those of agoraphobia. Beta-blockers rather than tranquillizers would be prescribed to deal with the physical symptoms of anxiety.

Final thoughts

Not all treatments work for everyone. If you have tried one type of treatment and it hasn't worked, you should discuss with your GP another type of treatment. This could be a psychological therapy, a different type of medication or following a self-help programme.

Medication combined with psychological therapy is believed to be the best method of dealing with anxiety disorders, including agoraphobia, and it is recommended that medication should not be used in isolation. In practice, however, this is not always easy to carry out. Unless you are able to afford to pay for psychological sessions privately, you may face a long wait to access psychological support on the NHS. In the meantime, you have to deal with the reality of living with agoraphobia. In contrast, a GP can prescribe antidepressants immediately. The lack of psychological services and long waiting lists are partly behind the rise in the number of antidepressant prescriptions issued.

If you are unable to access psychological therapy immediately, you could try following a programme of self-help at home. This would involve using cognitive behavioural techniques gradually to expose yourself to the situations of which you are afraid. These techniques are described in more detail in Chapter 10. You could also follow the cognitive behavioural therapy techniques in other self-help books, a list of which can be found in the Further reading section.

5

Complementary and alternative therapies

In recent years, the popularity of complementary medicine has grown enormously. Some people choose to use complementary therapies alongside medication or psychological treatments; others use the therapies instead of conventional treatment.

There is limited evidence for the efficacy of all complementary therapies at present but this doesn't mean they should be automatically ruled out. Lack of evidence means that they haven't yet been proved to be either helpful or unhelpful. Many people with anxiety have found benefits from using complementary therapies, such as helping them to relax. Relying on complementary therapies to 'cure' your agoraphobia is not advisable, as the evidence suggests it is unlikely to do so. But you may find that some of the therapies listed in this chapter help you manage your anxiety levels and learn to relax.

With the exception of herbal medicine, where greater care is needed, most complementary therapies have few or no side-effects. Therefore, they are worth a try to see if they are helpful. If you are housebound, it is worth explaining your difficulties to therapists and seeing whether they would consider a home visit. Some holistic therapists are 'mobile' and would be able to do this. Details of all the organizations and suppliers mentioned in this chapter can be found in the Useful addresses section at the end of the book.

Acupuncture

Acupuncture developed from traditional Chinese medicine, which dates back to the second century BC. It is based on the Chinese philosophy that our health is dependent on energy, called Qi, moving smoothly through a series of channels beneath the skin. This therapy works on the principle that Qi can become unbalanced and lead to illness.

Acupuncture involves inserting fine needles into specific parts of the body (the channels of Qi) to stimulate the body's own healing process and restore balance. It is a holistic therapy, which means it aims to treat the whole person, not just the specific symptom of illness. Acupuncture needles are very thin and do not hurt in the way that an injection does. The treatment is normally completely painless but some practitioners try to produce a sensation called 'de Qi' – a feeling of heaviness, soreness or warmth around the needle. Practitioners believe that this is a sign that the needles are in the right place.

Acupuncture is used widely both in the NHS and in private practice. It is most commonly used for chronic pain and muscular problems such as back pain. There is a lack of clinical research into acupuncture and only limited research on acupuncture and anxiety, but the available evidence has shown some positive findings.[7] This certainly suggests that more research should be carried out to find out how helpful this treatment is.

Acupuncture should only be carried out by a qualified practitioner and when done so is a very safe treatment. Serious side-effects are very rare. Anxiety and phobias are normally treated with a course of sessions, between six and eight treatments. If there is no improvement in your symptoms after this time, then it's unlikely to help. A full consultation should always take place before any treatment commences. To find a qualified practitioner contact either the British Medical Acupuncture Society or the British Acupuncture Council.

Aromatherapy

Aromatherapy uses essential oils which have been derived from plant material. These essential oils can be used in a variety of ways and they are either inhaled or massaged into the skin.

Aromatherapy is believed to change our mood by stimulating our sense of smell. Our sense of smell is very powerful and the body can distinguish thousands of different scents. Our sense of smell is believed to be linked to the area of the brain called the limbic system, which controls moods, memories and the ability to learn. Have you ever noticed that certain smells trigger specific memories, that the smell of food cooking makes you feel hungry or milk that has gone off makes you feel sick? Aromatherapy is designed to trigger a certain mood, such as relaxation.

Aromatherapy is being used on the NHS and the evidence points towards positive results for the short-term reduction of anxiety.[8] This means that it may not have a long-lasting effect but regular use could help you to reduce stress, if only for a short time. This makes it a good therapy to use alongside other methods of treatment.

You can book an aromatherapy massage in most beauty salons and you can also see an aromatherapist privately who could create a specific blend of oils for you. If you are unable to leave the house, you can still enjoy aromatherapy. You can buy pre-blended oils for relaxation and stress reduction over the internet. You can also buy single essential oils and create your own blend. Essential oils should never be placed directly on the skin, but should always be added to a carrier oil such as almond oil. Pre-blended massage oils are also available. Simple ways to introduce aromatherapy into your life are to add a few drops of oil to a warm bath, to your pillow or handkerchief. The oils can be burnt in an oil burner, or a pre-blended oil can be massaged into your skin.

The following oils are recommended for relieving anxiety:

- Lavender
- Geranium
- Valerian
- Spikenard
- Bergamot
- Neroli
- Vetiver
- Chamomile
- Sandalwood
- Melissa
- Frankincense

The choice of which oil to use is a personal one. However, if you don't like a particular scent, avoid it. It's best to use an oil which smells pleasant to you.

Autogenic therapy

Autogenic therapy was developed by the psychiatrist and neurologist Dr Johannes Schultz in the early years of the twentieth century. It has been practised since 1978 in the Royal London Homeopathic Hospital, part of the University College London Hospitals NHS Trust. The hospital has undertaken research into the therapy and found it to be effective for treating panic attacks, anxiety and insomnia.

Autogenic training is a series of mental exercises designed to bring about the relaxation response and switch off the body's fight or flight response. Autogenic means self-generated and techniques are designed to support the body's natural healing process. The exercises are taught by a practitioner over a number of weeks and practice at home is also needed. The British Autogenic Society provides a list of UK practitioners on its website.

Bach Flower Remedies

Bach Flower Remedies were developed by Dr Edward Bach between 1928 and 1935. They consist of 38 remedies made from flowering plants and trees, extracts of which are preserved in brandy. Bach Flower Remedies work on the philosophy that the body should heal itself and the remedies are designed to support the body to do so.

There is little evidence to support the effectiveness of Bach Flower Remedies and very limited clinical research. Sceptics say that positive results are down to the placebo effect, while practitioners believe that increasing veterinary use in animals counteracts this argument. As with many complementary therapies, it is a personal choice whether you decide to use it. It is safe to try alongside other treatments. There is a very small amount of alcohol in the remedies, a couple of drops over three weeks if you are using a standard treatment bottle daily.

The remedies can be used individually, or in combinations, up to a maximum of six or seven. There is only one pre-mixed combination called Rescue Remedy which uses five Bach Flower Remedies: Rock Rose, Cherry Plum, Star of Bethlehem, Clematis and Impatiens. Bach practitioners recommend Rescue Remedy for crisis situations such as a panic attack.

The Bach Flower Remedies normally used for anxiety are:

- Mimulus – for a fear of something you can name;
- Aspen – for panic attacks which come out of the blue for no reason and for unexplained fears;
- Rock Rose – for absolute terror and panic about something specific;
- Cherry Plum – for fear of losing control or doing something irrational or violent;
- Star of Bethlehem – for a shock or trauma that has happened in the past;
- Clematis – for faintness and fear of grounding (in some complementary therapies, grounding refers to being fully aware that you are in a physical body, and is used to stop people from feeling 'spaced out');
- Impatiens – for agitated and nervous feelings;
- Crab Apple – for a fear of germs and contamination and compulsive behaviour.

With Bach Flower Remedies you can self-prescribe and order online from the Bach Centre or have a private consultation with a Bach practitioner.

The Buteyko method

The Buteyko (pronounced 'bu-tay-ko') method is a series of special breathing exercises, techniques and lifestyle changes. The method was invented by a Russian medical scientist, Professor Konstantin Pavlovich Buteyko. It was originally designed to be used by asthmatics but it is now being used to treat dysfunctional breathing in individuals who do not have respiratory disease. The exercises address chronic hyperventilation. As this is a common problem in people with panic disorder, practitioners believe the method may help those with anxiety. So far research has only been undertaken in people with asthma and there is no clinical evidence on its effectiveness for panic attacks. The method should be taught by a Buteyko practitioner. It normally takes three to five sessions to learn the techniques and you need to practise them every day.

Herbal medicine

Herbal medicine is the use of plants in different forms to treat illness and promote good health. The use of plants as medicines has a long history and predates modern medicine. In fact, many modern medicines originate from plant sources: morphine, for example, comes from the opium poppy, and aspirin comes from willow bark. The difference between conventional medicine and herbal medicine is that, whereas conventional medicines contain an isolated active extract from a plant, herbalists use the whole plant. Herbalists also often use two or three herbs together. Herbal medicine is normally taken in the form of teas, tinctures or capsules of powdered herbs.

Herbal medicine is divided into two types: Western herbal medicine and Chinese herbal medicine. The two systems work in different ways, although both treat the whole person and aim to deal with the underlying causes of illness, rather than merely treating the specific symptoms brought about by an illness. Chinese herbal medicine is based on the concepts of Qi energy and yin and yang (the balance of two complementary yet opposing forces in the body and in the whole of nature). Western herbal medicine uses herbs to affect different body systems and herbs may be selected, for example, for their calming or anti-inflammatory properties.

Although herbal medicines are widely available in health stores it is not advisable to treat yourself. There is a myth that because herbs are 'natural' they are always safe. Herbs can be powerful and can also interact with other medications. Some herbs such as kava kava, which was used for anxiety, have been banned in the UK due to a possible link with liver damage. So if you are interested in using herbal medicine, perhaps as an alternative to conventional medication for anxiety, seek a consultation with a qualified medical herbalist. At the time of writing, the government was considering proposals to regulate a list of herbalists in the UK. In the meantime, it is best to consult a medical herbalist who is registered with the National Institute of Medical Herbalists (NIMH). Members of this body have undergone at least three years of training and follow a strict code of ethics. Members will normally display the letters MNIMH or FNIMH after their names.

Scientific evidence for the efficacy of herbalism as a whole is very limited and it isn't possible to draw clear conclusions from the few studies available. Clinical trials have been performed for specific herbs; however, these have often been compared to a placebo or a conventional drug.

The best-known evidence concerns the herb St John's wort, which has been shown to be effective for treating mild to moderate depression. It can also be used for anxiety, insomnia and seasonal affective disorder. This herb cannot be used alongside conventional antidepressant medication. Ginger has been shown to be effective for nausea and vomiting, feverfew for migraines and ginkgo for dementia. However, out of all the complementary therapies this is one that is best prescribed by a professional rather than by yourself.

Homeopathy

'Homeopathy' comes from the Greek words *homoios*, 'similar' and *pathos*, 'suffering' or 'disease'. Homeopathy aims to treat 'like with like'. You might be thinking that the last thing you want is more anxiety! However, homeopathy aims to restore balance and harmony within the body. The remedies use substances drawn from plants, animals and minerals which are so highly diluted that not one molecule of the original substance can be detected. There are five regulated pharmacies in the UK that produce homeopathic remedies. There are also currently five NHS homeopathic hospitals in England. Homeopathy has been practised in the UK for 200 years but its roots date back to ancient Greece. The system of homeopathy in use today was developed in 1796 by a doctor named Samuel Hahnemann.

Homeopathy is commonly used to treat depression, stress and anxiety. The evidence for its effectiveness is not clear as only a limited number of high-quality research studies have been carried out. However, surveys show that it is frequently used by people suffering from anxiety disorders. If you are interested in this therapy, you will need to see a homeopath for a detailed consultation. After this, he or she will prescribe a remedy, normally in the form of a tablet, powder or liquid. Contact the Society of Homeopaths for your nearest practitioner.

Reflexology

Reflexology is a therapy in which pressure is applied to specific points on the feet or hands. These 'reflex points' are believed to correspond with different parts of the body. The whole of the foot is covered in a treatment to bring the body into balance. Reflexology is believed to have been practised in Ancient Egypt, as a picture depicting the art has been found in a tomb dated 2350 BC.

Reflexology is not designed to diagnose illness or cure a medical problem – therapists believe that reflexology supports the body to heal itself. A session normally lasts one hour and a course of six to eight sessions is usually recommended.

Like other complementary therapies, reflexology is under-researched. There is very little evidence to support its effectiveness for treating any condition. One clinical trial in 2001 on the use of reflexology for irritable bowel syndrome (IBS) did show a significant reduction in anxiety levels, whereas no difference was noted for any other IBS symptoms. This study was on a small scale and the participants suffered from IBS, not an anxiety disorder; the authors of the study did however cite that further study should be undertaken on the use of reflexology for anxiety disorders as it initially showed a positive effect.[9] To find a qualified reflexologist in your area contact the Association of Reflexologists.

Complementary medicine can be useful on its own or as a supplement to any conventional therapy. Although the scientific evidence for its effectiveness is limited, this doesn't mean you won't experience any benefits. Anything which helps you to relax or reduce your anxiety levels is worth a try. We are all unique and respond in different ways to different therapies. Some people swear by a hot bath with lavender oil to unwind, while others wouldn't find it relaxing at all. Overcoming agoraphobia involves discovering what makes you anxious and what helps you to relax. By the time you have your agoraphobia under control, you should have a much better understanding of yourself. Take the time to try new things and discover what makes you feel calm and at peace.

6

Lifestyle changes

Most of the time we are so busy that we don't pay much attention to our lifestyles. But what we eat and drink, how much exercise we get and how well we sleep can all have a big effect on our anxiety levels. Many people with agoraphobia don't even realize that their lifestyle could be triggering panic attacks. Some experts believe that when panic attacks first start to occur, it is actually a warning sign from our body. Our body could be trying to tell us to slow down, reduce our stress levels or change the way we eat.

Think about your lifestyle at the time your panic attacks began. Were you under a lot of stress at work or at home? Were you living on takeaways and consuming a lot of alcohol and caffeine? Were you skipping on sleep or going through a physically demanding time? In susceptible individuals, all these factors can trigger panic attacks. The good news is that making changes to your lifestyle can help reduce your anxiety levels and overcome your agoraphobia. This chapter is designed to help you explore your lifestyle and see if there are any changes you can make that will help you feel less anxious.

Avoiding stimulants

The first area to consider is whether you are over-stimulating your body. Someone with agoraphobia is likely already to have high levels of anxiety and does not need any extra stimulation. The most common stimulants are nicotine, alcohol, recreational drugs and caffeine.

Nicotine

The dangers of smoking are well known but, in addition, too much nicotine stimulates the body, increasing stress and anxiety. If you smoke, you may think that a cigarette helps you to relax and calm down. However, any relaxing effect is likely to be due to the fact you are breathing deeply and that you associate a cigarette with relaxation. It may not be easy to quit smoking overnight, but instead you could try reducing your intake of nicotine. You may also wish to consider nicotine replacement patches; see Useful addresses for organizations that can help.

Alcohol

Alcohol is another deceptive stimulant. When you first drink alcohol it has a sedative effect – you may have found that you can only get through a social occasion, for example, with the help of alcohol. However, as your body later metabolizes the alcohol it becomes a stimulant and, combined with a hangover, can greatly heighten your anxiety and trigger panic attacks. If you have ever become drunk in order to deal with anxiety, you will be familiar with this feeling of being 'on edge' the following day.

But because of the initial sedative effects of alcohol, there is a link between anxiety and alcohol abuse. It is estimated that between 16 and 25 per cent of people with anxiety have alcohol problems, while one survey found that between 22 and 68.7 per cent of people taking part in alcohol programmes also had an anxiety disorder.[10]

Sometimes people with an alcohol problem can develop an anxiety disorder as a direct result of their alcohol abuse. In other cases, an anxiety disorder is at the root of the problem and the alcohol abuse has arisen in an attempt by the person to mask his or her anxiety. You can easily see how alcohol could be used by someone with agoraphobia to help them deal with frightening situations. However, if you do this you run a very high risk of developing a second problem, alcoholism, as well as your original agoraphobia. In order to get the same effects from alcohol, more and more will be needed and the very upsetting withdrawal symptoms will have to be endured or more alcohol consumed – creating a vicious circle.

Only you know whether you are using alcohol to deal with your agoraphobia, or if your agoraphobia has developed as a result of abusing alcohol. Either way, any treatment should deal with both issues. If you have specific problems with use of or withdrawal from alcohol, you need to get help; while you will need further treatment to deal with your agoraphobia. Your GP is still your best port of call to arrange help and there are a number of organizations that provide support for alcohol problems (see Useful addresses).

In the long run, using alcohol is not an effective strategy for dealing with agoraphobia and is best avoided until you have recovered. In addition, alcohol can sometimes have an effect on any medication you take. If you are taking medication, you should discuss with your doctor whether you can drink alcohol, and how much you can drink.

Recreational drugs

Recreational drugs can also trigger anxiety disorders. Some drugs such as cocaine, ecstasy and amphetamines can produce symptoms of anxiety during use or withdrawal. Studies show that panic attacks and anxiety reactions can occur during cannabis and cocaine use.[11] Like alcohol, recreational drugs are sometimes used to mask the symptoms of an existing anxiety disorder, and as with alcohol a vicious cycle of anxiety and drug use can occur. If you are using recreational drugs, you will need to stop in order to overcome your agoraphobia and panic attacks.

You may need some help from your doctor to stop using these drugs. Sometimes your doctor can prescribe medications to deal with the effects of withdrawal. Your doctor can also put you in touch with any specialist help you need to stop using drugs. Once this has been addressed, you will need further help, perhaps medication and psychotherapy as well as the self-help measures described in this book, to tackle your agoraphobia.

Caffeine

Caffeine is another stimulating and addictive substance, despite its widespread use and acceptance. Caffeine is found naturally in tea leaves, coffee beans, cola nuts and cocoa beans. It is also added to some energy drinks and over-the-counter medicines, such as painkillers and cold and flu medicines. Caffeine stimulates the central nervous system (the brain and spinal cord), making the heart beat faster. Caffeine is believed to work by blocking a natural sedative in the brain, tricking the body to stay alert for longer.

For someone who is already sensitive to anxiety, anything which speeds up the heart rate, triggering even more stress responses, is not a good idea. So it's beneficial to look at how much caffeine you are consuming and how you can reduce it. Over a week, monitor how many cups of tea, coffee or hot chocolate you drink, how many glasses of cola you drink and how many bars of chocolate you eat and if you take any painkillers containing caffeine. You do not have to eliminate caffeine completely and never eat a bar of chocolate! But if you are consuming a lot of caffeine, or even a moderate amount, cutting right down can have a big effect on your anxiety level.

You can switch to decaffeinated coffee and tea, though despite the name these products are not completely caffeine free. Or try herbal teas for a completely caffeine-free hot drink (beware of green tea, which contains caffeine). Chocolate contains less caffeine than tea or coffee, so it can still be enjoyed in moderation; milk chocolate has less caffeine than dark chocolate. And you can simply avoid any painkillers that contain caffeine.

To give you an idea of how much caffeine a particular drink contains, a cup of instant coffee has 75mg while a cup of brewed coffee has 100mg. A cup of tea has 50mg and a can of cola can have up to 40mg. A 50g bar of plain chocolate has up to 20mg, a milk chocolate bar around 7mg. A cup of hot chocolate has 5mg and a cup of green tea has 4mg. The amount of caffeine added to medicines or energy drinks should be stated on the packaging.

The key is moderation, although pregnant women are advised to consume no more than 300mg a day of caffeine. But if you find that consuming caffeine increases your anxiety levels, you may decide to cut it out altogether. Or you may find that a chocolate bar or glass of cola has no effect on your anxiety, while drinking a few cups of coffee does. The aim is not to make you feel deprived, but to use every tool you have to tackle your agoraphobia.

If you are consuming a moderate to high amount of caffeine every day (over 300mg), cutting out caffeine altogether may cause some withdrawal effects. These include a headache or a fuzzy head, or feeling more tired than usual. Drinking plenty of water, at least eight glasses a day, will help your body with the detoxification process and may prevent headaches. If you don't think you can cut out all caffeine suddenly, you can gradually decrease the amount. This will help prevent withdrawal effects. Any such effects should last no longer than a week, and if you've been consuming a lot of caffeine, you should see a reduction in your anxiety levels.

The right nutrition

There is a growing belief that the foods we eat can affect our moods. Adapting our diet is another weapon we can use to overcome agoraphobia as well as improving our general health.

Scientific evidence about the relationship between food and mood is slowly starting to emerge, but it is a subject that is hard to test. This is because scientific studies need to show that any particular treatment works whether or not we believe it will. In most studies a group of people will take the medicine being tested while another group takes a placebo (a dummy pill), and neither the participants nor the researchers know which is which. This helps to remove any bias, because if we believe something will work, it is more likely to work.

If we are testing foods, though, it's quite hard to create pretend food or to hide from the people involved in the study what food they are being given. Putting foods into capsules or feeding foods directly into people's stomachs when they are in hospital are two possible strategies, but as you can imagine these are not without their pitfalls.

But the anecdotal evidence is growing, and you can monitor your symptoms to see if changes in nutrition help you. The best way to monitor any changes is to start a food and symptom diary. Before making any changes, keep a diary of everything you eat and drink, and if possible of roughly when you eat. You may find it easier to keep a notebook with you and make notes after you have eaten. Also, record how you felt – whether you had any panic attacks, when they occurred, whether you experienced high levels of anxiety or periods of calmness or tiredness, and so on. The idea is to build up a greater awareness of what we are consuming and how we feel, and see if we can spot any links.

It can be hard to remember what we eat on a day-to-day basis, which is why a food and symptom diary can be really helpful. You might notice that on one day you consumed a lot of caffeine or sugary foods and felt more anxious. You might see that you are eating a lot of one particular food group and not much of another. You need this awareness to help you analyse what could be a problem in your diet.

Follow a balanced diet that includes foods from the major groups of proteins and carbohydrates, as well as fruit and vegetables. In order to get the vitamins and minerals we need, we have to eat a variety of foods, not just the same types every day. It is recommended that we should eat at least five portions of fruit and vegetables a day (a portion is about the size of your fist), as well as drinking at least eight glasses of water a day. Most of us do not drink enough water and this is one simple and free way to improve our well-being straight away. It is also important to reduce any stimulants, as described above.

You may want to consider eating foods that are thought to reduce anxiety levels. There are two ways of doing this: first, to eat more foods which are believed to increase serotonin levels, and second, to maintain an even blood sugar balance.

Mood-enhancing foods

Experts believe that people suffering from agoraphobia, panic disorders and depression have low levels of serotonin, a neurotransmitter in the brain that affects mood, behaviour, appetite and sleep. As we saw in Chapter 4, antidepressants work by blocking the reabsorption (reuptake) of serotonin and therefore increasing its level. However, serotonin is made naturally in the brain from tryptophan, an amino acid found in foods that contain protein. Protein cannot be produced by the body and has to be obtained from our food. So eating foods rich in tryptophan is one way of increasing the amount of serotonin your brain produces.

For tryptophan to be absorbed by the brain it needs carbohydrate foods. The carbohydrates help tryptophan to cross the blood–brain barrier and be converted into serotonin. Some nutritional experts believe that carbohydrate cravings are the body's way of trying to correct low levels of serotonin. So a food containing tryptophan should be accompanied by or followed by carbohydrates. Care needs to be taken when choosing a carbohydrate – if you eat unrefined carbohydrates (examples include biscuits, cakes, white bread and pasta) you could find yourself on a blood-sugar rollercoaster. How to choose the right carbohydrate is covered later in this chapter.

According to Amanda Geary, founder of the Food and Mood project with the charity Mind (see Useful addresses), the best sources of tryptophan are:

- chicken – 100g contains 360mg of tryptophan
- turkey – 100g contains 340mg
- tuna – 85g contains 280mg
- salmon – 85g contains 260mg
- kidney beans – 170g contains 180mg
- rolled oats – 85g contains 175mg
- lentils – 200g contains 160mg
- chickpeas – 200g contains 140mg
- pumpkin seeds – 30g contains 120mg
- sunflower seeds – 30g contains 100mg

Other mood-enhancing foods are those that release endorphins, the chemicals responsible for the body's natural 'high', also released during exercise. It is thought that endorphins are released by foods containing phenylethlamine, one of which is chocolate. The problem with eating these types of foods to lift your mood is that you can end in an addictive cycle, needing to eat more and more to get the same feeling. Foods containing phenylethlamine are normally high in sugar and/or fat, so they are likely to cause your blood sugar to drop, as well as carrying the health risks associated with eating foods rich in calories and low in nutrients. For this reason, it is better to eat tryptophan-rich foods to get your 'mood enhancing' fix and the effects will be longer lasting.

The right fats

Essential fatty acids (EFAs) are also very important for mental health as they are needed to facilitate the release of neurotransmitters in the brain. Some studies have shown that a deficiency in EFAs is linked to psychiatric problems and that increasing the levels of EFAs helps to reduce symptoms. Other studies indicate that taking EFAs alongside antidepressants enhances their effect in treating the mental health problem.

There are two types of EFAs, Omega-3 and Omega-6. Omega-3 is found in raw nuts and seeds; green leafy vegetables; oily fish such as salmon, mackerel, herring, sardines, fresh tuna, trout, pilchards; unsaturated vegetable oils such as sesame oil, grapeseed oil and soybean oil. Omega-6 is found in fresh deepwater fish, fish oils and some vegetable oils such as walnut oil and flaxseed oil. The richest source of Omega-3 and Omega-6 is found in oily fish and it is recommended that you eat three portions of this a week.

An alternative is to take a EFA supplement, which can be purchased from a health shop (see Useful addresses for mail order details). This is also the best way of ensuring that you get the right balance of Omega-3 and Omega-6, as the brain needs both. If you are allergic to fish or are vegetarian, flax seeds provide Omega-3, while walnuts, sunflower seeds, hemp seeds, soybeans, wheatgerm and evening primrose oil provide Omega-6.

Other supplements

It is generally accepted that the best way to get vitamins is from a balanced diet. However, suffering from anxiety for a long period of time can deplete the body's resources. In addition to an EFA supplement, you may also want to consider a B vitamin complex and a zinc supplement. B vitamins are important for mood and energy levels; vitamin B6 in particular helps metabolize EFAs and helps the production of serotonin. It is common to be deficient in zinc and our need for zinc increases during times of anxiety. Zinc is also required for metabolizing EFAs and for producing serotonin. Low levels of zinc have also been associated with anxiety and depression. So the most important supplements for anxiety disorders are an EFA supplement containing Omega-3 and Omega-6, vitamin B6 or B complex and zinc.

Foods rich in B vitamins include bananas, avocados, beans, fish, lentils, meat, milk, eggs, nuts and seeds. Sources of zinc include brazil nuts; walnuts; sunflower, sesame and pumpkin seeds; lamb; oysters and herring. Zinc is also good for building up immunity, which may be under strain due to high levels of anxiety.

Maintaining blood sugar balance

Taking control of blood sugar balance is one of the most effective ways of managing your mood and energy levels. Many of us are taken on a daily blood sugar rollercoaster ride through eating the wrong types of foods. Maintaining an even blood sugar balance is especially important for people with anxiety, as low blood sugar episodes can trigger a panic attack. Low levels of blood glucose can also cause fatigue, irritability, aggression, trembling, nervousness, sweating, dizziness and a fast heart rate. Many of these symptoms are similar to those experienced during a panic attack, so it's no surprise that low blood sugar can trigger a panic attack.

Blood sugar refers to the amount of glucose circulating in the bloodstream. The body uses glucose for food and energy; it is collected from the liver where it is stored as glycogen. The body has its own control mechanism for maintaining an even blood sugar balance. Blood sugar is normally between 80mg and 180mg per 100ml of blood. Two hormones control blood sugar: insulin and adrenalin.

When blood sugar levels are high, insulin is secreted by the pancreas to stop any more glycogen being broken down in the liver and encouraging the muscles to store glucose. When the body does not produce enough insulin, blood sugar levels get too high and hyperglycaemia (diabetes) occurs. When too much insulin is produced, blood sugar levels fall too low, causing hypoglycaemia. When blood sugar runs low, adrenalin is released, stimulating the liver to break down and release stored glycogen. As adrenalin is one of the stress hormones that trigger feelings of panic, it is especially important for people with anxiety disorders to maintain even blood sugar.

If you regularly experience panic attacks, your body will be using up its energy supplies more quickly than normal. Not only will this make you feel more tired, you may need shorter gaps between meals. The traditional three meals a day may not be suitable; small meals or snacks every two to three hours may be a better way of maintaining even blood sugar.

During an attack of low blood sugar, the quickest way to relieve the symptoms is to eat or drink something high in glucose or sugar such as a glucose tablet, a glucose drink, or a sugary snack like sweets, biscuits or chocolate. It is fine to do this during an attack, as most people will want relief from the symptoms as soon as possible. However, this is not the way to manage or prevent the situation in the long term. Instead, change to a diet rich in protein, and low in sugary or refined carbohydrates. In fact, regular low blood sugar attacks are a sign that you need to include more protein-rich foods in your diet.

There has been a lot of publicity recently about GI (glycaemic index) diets. Using these can help you manage your blood sugar levels very effectively. The glycaemic index is a way of measuring the effect food has on your blood sugar level. Pure glucose can be absorbed undigested into the bloodstream, producing the maximum effect on blood sugar levels in the shortest amount of time; this gives glucose a maximum score of 100 on the glycaemic index. All foods are given a rating from 0 to 100, depending on how quickly they raise blood sugar. In order to maintain even blood sugar, the general rule is to consume foods that have a low GI, or combine foods with a higher GI with those that have a lower GI.

When blood sugar is raised quickly, insulin is released to bring it down, meaning you will soon experience a drop in your blood sugar. This yo-yo effect can be avoided by eating foods with a lower GI index. Carbohydrates can often have a high GI but they shouldn't be cut out altogether. They are a very necessary food group, important for processing tryptophan which produces serotonin, as described earlier in this chapter. Unrefined, starchy carbs tend to have the highest GI; for example white rice, baked potatoes, chips, French baguettes and bread. Lower GI alternatives include rye bread, oat cake biscuits, pitta bread, barley, quinoa, basmati rice, sweet potato, buckwheat and wholemeal spaghetti.

See Further Reading and Useful addresses for resources that will enable you to explore GI diets in more detail.

Exercise

Exercise is generally seen as a positive thing, but some caution is needed when you have agoraphobia.

If you are housebound or restricted in your routine, you may not be getting as much exercise as you used to. You may feel drained and lethargic as the result of experiencing high levels of anxiety and may feel that exercise is the last thing on your mind.

Exercise can be very beneficial, as it can lift our mood by releasing endorphins. It can also use up any excess energy, improving the quality of our sleep. But there is a fine balance between exercising too little and too much. If you have been inactive for a while, you should check with your GP that it is OK to start exercising.

When we exercise we are putting a stress on our body, and our body responds by releasing the stress hormone cortisol. If you are experiencing frequent panic attacks or high levels of anxiety, your levels of cortisol are likely to be high already. So strenuous exercise may actually have a detrimental effect on your well-being and may not help to decrease your anxiety. Cardiovascular exercises such as running or aerobics are the types of exercise most likely to release cortisol. Exercise is most likely to be beneficial if you allow yourself plenty of rest periods, allowing time where you are relaxed and not releasing cortisol due to stress. Even elite athletes build rest periods into their training schedules. However, complete inactivity is not helpful either, so it is best to do gentle exercise when your anxiety levels are high. The intensity of the exercise can be gradually increased as you feel less stressed and anxious.

The best forms of exercise for anxiety are those which also aim to calm the mind. Yoga, Pilates or t'ai chi are all good choices, and can easily be practised at home with the aid of a DVD (see Useful addresses for mail-order details). Gentle walking on a treadmill or using an exercise bike at home may also be helpful, but take care not to over-exert yourself. To make sure you don't, try the 'talk test'. This test simply means that while you are exercising you should be able to talk easily and hold a conversation. If you are unable to do so, you need to slow down or stop until you can talk comfortably again. If you experience dizziness or pain, always stop.

Dental care

If you have been experiencing high levels of anxiety, extra care is needed in your dental routine. A study showed that women who suffer from stress, depression and exhaustion experience higher levels of plaque and gum inflammation.[12] Experts believe that this is due to stress hormones triggering the release of inflammatory cytokines. Cytokines are a protein produced by white blood cells and they prevent the immune system from doing its job properly. These cytokines may cause gum inflammation and slow down the body's healing process so that even cuts and grazes take longer to heal.[13]

Another effect of stress hormones is the reduction of saliva in the mouth, as all fluids and energy are directed to the muscles needed for the fight or flight response. This reduced saliva production can cause increased growth of bacteria in the mouth.

Practising your regular relaxation exercise will help, as will increasing your intake of immune-boosting foods. As suggested earlier in this chapter, you may also want to consider taking a supplement for your immune system containing vitamin C and zinc.

Managing your dental care

Another way to prevent and manage gum disease is to have a good dental care routine. If your gums bleed when you brush them, this is a sign that your gums are inflamed (this is called gingivitis), a condition that will lead to gum disease if not treated. Brushing your teeth twice a day is essential; if you are mostly at home, you may want to brush your teeth after every meal. The type of toothbrush you use is important. Investing in an electronic or ideally a sonic toothbrush is worthwhile, as they are proven to remove more plaque than a normal toothbrush. You should follow brushing with mouthwash; choose one that is alcohol free to avoid irritating inflamed gums. You should also floss at least once a day. Following a strict oral care routine like this should reduce bleeding gums or prevent them occurring.

If you do have bleeding gums, there are mouthwashes available to buy over the counter for gingivitis. Using a course of these, in combination with a strict brushing and flossing routine, should help. Ideally, you should visit your dentist for a check-up every six months, but this may not be easy if you are housebound. If you have tried all the self-help measures suggested and your gums are still bleeding and inflamed, a trip to your dentist will be necessary to treat the condition properly. Sometimes antibiotics are prescribed and dentists can remove the build-up of plaque deposits that brushing alone cannot, helping reduce gum inflammation. If you are housebound, a trip to your dentist should be a high priority as soon as you feel you can manage it. Taking someone with you may help to relieve your anxiety.

Inflamed and bleeding gums are not pleasant; they can cause bad breath and a nasty taste in the mouth as well as soreness on the gums. It may not be your highest priority when overcoming agoraphobia but it is worth trying to maintain good gum health. Many people are nervous about visiting a dentist and most dentists are very understanding about this. The National Phobics Society has produced an information sheet for those suffering from dental phobia, which may be useful if your fear of the dentist is a separate issue from your agoraphobia.

Seasonal Affective Disorder (SAD)

SAD is a winter depression that normally affects people between September and April. It is estimated that half a million people in the UK are affected every winter. There is no established link between anxiety disorders and SAD but some people with agoraphobia find their symptoms worse in the winter. Symptoms of SAD include sleep problems, feelings of lethargy, cravings for carbohydrates and sweet foods, loss of interest in sex, feelings of depression, mood swings, increased anxiety and the desire to avoid social contact.

The exact cause of SAD is still unknown but experts believe that it may be linked to seasonal variation in the release of serotonin and the increased production of the hormone melatonin. During daylight hours, hardly any melatonin is released; but when night falls, our pineal gland starts to release melatonin to help us feel tired and sleepy. SAD is also extremely rare in people who live within 30 degrees of the equator, possibly indicating that long hours of daylight prevent the condition. It also means that those of us who live outside 30 degrees of the equator are at risk of SAD during our winter months.

Winter may have no effect on your agoraphobia at all. But it's worth keeping an eye out for it and seeing if you find it harder to get outside during winter. If you do think SAD is affecting you there are a couple of different treatments you can try. Light therapy and antidepressants have been shown to be effective. Light therapy involves sitting in front of a bright light. While normal lighting is about 200–500 lux, a SAD lamp is 2500 lux (a bright summer's day can be 100,000 lux!). See Useful addresses for suppliers of these lamps. Simple measures like wrapping up warm and going outside on a winter's day can also help.

Sleep

Along with other people experiencing anxiety, those with agoraphobia can sometimes have problems with sleep. You may find it hard to relax enough to fall asleep or you may wake up in the middle of night having a panic attack. It can be particularly frightening to be experiencing panic attacks during the middle of night in the dark, when it seems as if the whole world is peacefully asleep.

If you regularly have problems falling asleep, try to explore why that is and whether anything in your bedtime routine can be changed. Do you need some distraction from your thoughts to stop you dwelling on your anxiety? Do you lie awake 'listening in' to your body and panicking about every new or unusual sensation you feel?

If this is the case, it may be worth experimenting with reading a book at bedtime, listening to an audio story or watching TV in bed. Some people find having a TV on in the background helps them sleep, although others find it keeps them awake. Practising your breathing and relaxation exercises before going to sleep will be helpful as it should help to relax your body. Does a warm bath help you relax? Or a soothing herbal tea such as camomile? Many people find the scent of lavender soothing and a few drops of this essential oil could be sprinkled on your bed sheets.

Are you eating any particular foods which could be keeping you awake? You should avoid stimulating or spicy foods, alcohol and caffeine after seven o'clock. Make sure you go to bed when you feel tired and empty your bladder. But don't go to bed hungry. You shouldn't eat a heavy meal before going to bed as your body's digestive system slows down at night and eating a big meal at night will keep your body awake. But if you're hungry at bedtime, a light snack such as a banana and a cup of warm milk will be soothing.

If you cannot sleep, it is best to get up and out of the bedroom. Tossing and turning all night will only increase your anxiety. Go to a different room and read, or do some light housework until you feel sleepy, then return to your bed. Try to get up at the same time every day. If you sleep in, this will prevent you falling asleep at a reasonable hour the next night.

Coping with panic attacks at night

If you tend to wake up in the middle of the night with a panic attack, plan how to cope with these episodes. Is there a CD track you can listen to that will help you calm down, or a relaxation exercise? You may want to get out of bed and stay in a different room until you have calmed down. Is there some reassuring information you could write down for yourself to read in the night? In the middle of the night, it's easy to forget how to challenge negative thoughts and to remember how to relax your body. By leaving yourself some night-time instructions you can try to reassure yourself that this feeling of panic will pass. You may also find that going to another room and switching on a light helps your panic fade away. Frightening thoughts can seem worse in darkness.

Sometimes when we are in the early stages of sleep, different bodily sensations can occur. These are perfectly harmless but may feel very frightening to someone who is sensitized to their bodily sensations because of panic attacks. These sensations might be jerks or a sensation of falling which wakes you up suddenly. Occasionally, what is known as sleep paralysis can occur: we experience wakefulness but cannot move our body. When we are asleep our body is 'paralysed' to stop us acting out our dreams; while this sensation is unpleasant, it is harmless and quickly passes.

If your anxiety levels are very high and you are agitated, you may find it hard to lie still enough to go to sleep. In this case, see your doctor as he or she will be able to prescribe medication to reduce your agitation and help you sleep. In the next chapter, we will look at some further changes you can make to help your body and mind relax.

7

Learning to relax

The secret of overcoming agoraphobia is teaching yourself to relax in the situations you are afraid of. Of course, although it's easy to practise relaxing in the safety of your own home, it's quite another thing to try to relax in the middle of a busy supermarket.

This is why you need to equip yourself with the tools to cope with the anxiety you feel when you leave your place of safety. It isn't enough to tell yourself just to relax, not when you have been feeling so anxious for so long. You probably automatically associate going out with feeling anxious and your body may tense up without you even realizing it. As you put on your coat and prepare to leave the house, you may already have built up so much tension in your body that the slightest thought, fear or sensation will either stop you from going out at all or send you running back shortly after you leave home. It's easy to say 'Not today, maybe I'll get there tomorrow'; before you know it, weeks can go by without you stepping out of the house. To go outside with confidence, you need to learn how to relax.

True relaxation is more than just putting your feet up on the sofa and watching TV. You need to learn how to relax every set of muscles in your body and how to breathe slowly and calmly. You need to learn how to spot the difference between a tense body or muscle and a relaxed one. So when you prepare to go outside, you will actually be aware of your muscles becoming tense, of your breathing speeding up, and you can deliberately relax your body and slow down your breathing. It's impossible to panic if your body is completely relaxed.

If you're reading this in the comfort of your own home, you may be thinking 'I don't need to do this, I feel relaxed', or 'There's no point, this is too simple to help me and it's never going to work'. Learning to relax your body and control how you breathe appears very simple, but in fact it takes some time to truly reap the benefits. As I've said many times already, there isn't some magic cure or special treatment that is going to take away your fears overnight. But the techniques in this chapter are effective coping tools that will help you manage your anxiety levels and eventually help you control your panic when you step outside.

Breathing calmly

The first technique we are going to look at is how to breathe calmly and stop or avoid hyperventilation. As we saw in Chapter 3, when you begin to panic your body automatically starts overbreathing (hyperventilating). The unpleasant sensations you experience because of overbreathing cause further anxiety, leading to even more anxiety-related symptoms. This becomes a vicious cycle. Many people, as soon as they start to become anxious, immediately overbreathe.

But, if you can slow your breathing rate down, these symptoms will pass and your body's stress response will also start to slow down. A panic attack has to end, it cannot last for ever, and you can control when it ends.

One way to overcome hyperventilation during a panic attack is to breathe into a paper bag. Hold it tightly over your mouth and nose while breathing. Overbreathing causes too much oxygen to build up and too much carbon dioxide to leave the body. But your body needs carbon dioxide to reduce the levels of oxygen. When you breathe into a paper bag, the carbon dioxide builds up inside the bag and as you breathe in you reinhale the carbon dioxide. This will restore the balance between oxygen and carbon dioxide, and as result stop those unpleasant sensations. If you have no paper bag to hand or it isn't practical to use one, you could try breathing into tightly cupped hands. You could also try holding your breath for 10–15 seconds a few times, which will stop carbon dioxide from leaving your body too quickly. But by using a specific breathing and relaxation technique, you can start controlling your anxiety more effectively in the long term.

Before I explain the exercise in full, it is important to say that you will need to practise it many times at home. You need to be completely familiar with it before using it in a situation you find difficult. The exercise should become automatic, almost second nature. When you are very scared it can be hard to think of anything except getting out of the situation that is causing your fear. This is why you need to be totally familiar with the exercise to get the maximum benefit from it in anxiety-provoking situations. In Chapter 10, we look at how to expose yourself gradually to the situations you have been avoiding. This exercise will be one of the tools you will be using.

Luckily, the exercise is very easy to carry out and you can practise it pretty much anywhere. You can also buy specific breathing or deep relaxation CDs (see Useful addresses). Although listening to a CD is useful, you may not be able to do so every time you are out of the house. By all means use it at home, but make sure you practise so that you are able to carry out the techniques without it.

Relaxed breathing exercise

Even though breathing is automatic, there is actually a right and a wrong way to breathe. When we feel anxious, we take shallow, rapid breaths from our chest. We can fall into the habit of breathing shallowly because of high levels of anxiety but also for lifestyle reasons. If our posture is poor or if we slump in our seat, this also causes us to breathe more shallowly from our chest.

The correct breathing method is to breathe slowly and deeply from the bottom of the stomach. The best way to see whether you are breathing correctly is to lie flat on your stomach and rest your hands on your belly: your hands should rise and fall as you breathe.

To practise the breathing exercise, find a time when you do not feel anxious and will not be disturbed. Lie down and loosen any tight clothing. Make yourself as comfortable as possible and close your eyes.

- Be still and focus on your breathing. Feel your breath going in and out and let all other thoughts drift from your mind.
- Place your hands across your stomach, with your fingertips touching.
- Take a slow, deep breath in through your nose. It should be a smooth breath without gasping or gulping. As you breathe in, your fingertips should move apart. Your stomach should inflate like a balloon.
- Let your breath out slowly and gradually. As you do this your fingertips should touch again.
- Continue breathing in to the count of four and gently exhaling to the count of four: in – 2 – 3 – 4; out – 2 – 3 – 4. You may find it hard to do this at first but keep persevering. The aim is to retrain your body to take slow, deep breaths and inflate your lungs fully instead of quick shallow breaths.
- While you are breathing, you may wish to imagine a calming colour or peaceful scene such as a beach or waterfall. This will help your body associate breathing slowly with feeling calm.

Once you have got used to the technique, you will not need to lie down to practise it. You can practise it anywhere – walking, sitting, in the car, or whenever you start to feel nervous and feel your breathing speeding up.

Relaxation

The second technique we are going to look at is relaxing every part of your body. Relaxation is the opposite of tension. When you are anxious, your body's muscles become tense and taut. If you are anxious for long periods of time, this can leave you exhausted, your muscles aching. You may have spent so much time feeling anxious that you may not even realize how tense your body is. This relaxation exercise teaches you how to spot when your body is becoming tense and how to relax it.

The technique I am about to describe is called progressive relaxation therapy. This routine was developed by Dr Edward Jacobsen in the 1930s;[14] it was designed as a systematic way of relaxing the major muscle groups in the body, and to help people spot when their muscles are becoming tense and to know how to relax them instead. You may find that you don't feel fully relaxed when you first carry out this exercise. This is perfectly normal. It takes time to learn a new skill and this is one that is worth sticking at, as many people have found it helpful for controlling their anxiety.

Practise this exercise every day, ideally twice, until you can relax any set of muscles at any time. Use the technique whenever you feel tension building in any part of your body.

Deep relaxation exercise

When you first start to practise this exercise, find a quiet place where you can either sit or lie down undisturbed.

- *Hands and forearms.* Clench your fists as tightly as you can. Hold your fists tense to the count of 10, and relax. Can you feel the difference between being tense and relaxed?
- *Upper arms.* Tense these muscles by bending your arms and try to touch your shoulders with your wrists. Count to 10; relax.
- *Back of arms.* Tense the muscle by straightening your arms as hard as you can. Count to 10; relax.
- *Shoulders.* Shrug your shoulders tightly into your neck. Count to 10; relax.
- *Neck.* Press your head back as far as you can. Count to 10; relax.
- *Forehead.* Raise your eyebrows as far as you can. Count to 10; relax.
- *Eyes.* Frown and squeeze your eyes tightly shut. Count to 10; relax.

- *Jaw.* Clench your teeth together as hard as you can. Count to 10; relax.
- *Tongue and throat.* Press your tongue against the roof of your mouth as hard as you can. Count to 10; relax.
- *Lips.* Press your lips together as hard as you can. Count to 10; relax.
- *Chest.* Take a deep breath in and hold it. Count to 10; relax.
- *Stomach.* Tense your stomach muscles as hard as you can. Count to 10; relax.
- *Lower back.* Arch your back up and clench your buttock muscles together as hard as you can. Count to 10; relax.
- *Legs and feet.* Straighten your legs tightly and point your toes down. Count to 10; relax.

The aim of this exercise is for you to notice the difference between a tense muscle and a relaxed one. When you are in a situation where you feel anxious, you can use this tool to help you. When you start to feel a muscle group becoming tense, you can simply tense it consciously, hold the tension for the count of 10 and then relax the muscle group.

Tips for relaxation

A common problem that occurs when carrying out relaxation exercises is falling asleep – though this may not be a problem for you if you are using the exercise at night. If you are carrying out the exercise during the day and wish to avoid falling asleep, you could try sitting up instead of lying down.

Sometimes worrying thoughts can enter your mind when you are trying to relax. The best way of dealing with this is to ignore them and not to dwell on them. Let the thoughts flow through your mind and out again. You may want to listen to some soothing music while you practise relaxing, or concentrate on hearing all the sounds around you – it is surprising what you can hear when you stop and let your sense of hearing stretch out! Concentrating on sound can help you not to dwell on your thoughts.

Occasionally, as we concentrate on relaxing the body we may feel odd sensations. Again, ignore these, and focus on doing the exercise. Any odd sensations will soon disappear as you get used to carrying out the exercise. Make sure that you are not hyperventilating during the exercise and are taking slow, deep breaths from your stomach, not shallow, fast breaths from your chest. This will ensure that you gain the maximum benefit from relaxation and are not adding any tension to your body.

Creative visualization

In addition to the exercises outlined here, you may also want to try creative visualization. This is a type of meditation which uses positive imagery. It can be helpful for relaxation and for dealing with negative or frightening images which pop up in our minds when we're anxious.

One technique is to imagine a protective bubble around you in a calming colour like blue. Imagine that this bubble completely surrounds your body and keeps you safe. Visualize any negative, scary or frightening thoughts coming towards the bubble and simply bouncing off. Inside your bubble you feel safe, calm and protected. This bubble is with you wherever you go and nothing negative can pass through it.

If you often feel light-headed or struggle with unreality then you could try a grounding visualization. Sit with your feet flat on the floor or stand still. Then imagine tree roots stretching out from the soles of your feet reaching right down into the core of the earth. When you imagine these roots, use a deep red or brown colour for the roots or imagine yourself bathed in a red or brown light. Whenever you feel light-headed, immediately picture these roots from your feet connecting you to the earth's core.

See Useful addresses for more details on where to find creative visualization CDs.

8

Spotting your triggers

Do you have any idea what it is that triggers your panic attacks? What is it that makes you run home in terror? What starts this uneasy feeling that makes it impossible to relax and enjoy yourself when you leave your home? It may feel as if your panic attacks strike you completely out of the blue, or that simply stepping outside is the trigger for a panic attack. But if you analyse a panic attack in detail, you may discover that there were actually a number of triggers which led up to it.

When you are feeling anxious and worrying about what is going to happen next, it's very difficult to step back and analyse what is happening. This chapter explores how you can find out exactly what is making you panic and how you can tackle these triggers of anxiety.

What triggers a panic attack?

As we saw in Chapter 3, panic attacks are triggered by your body's alarm system when there is no real danger to your survival. However, if we take a closer look at a panic attack we can start to identify what these triggers are.

Look at these two examples:

You start to get a headache. You think: 'I'm getting a headache, I think I'll take some painkillers and go to bed.'

You start to get a headache. You think: 'Oh no, I'm getting a headache. It must be a sign of a brain tumour. I'm going to die.'

Can you see how the second example could trigger a panic attack? In both the examples above, there is the same physical trigger – the headache. However, there are two different approaches to dealing with it.

In the first example, the person accepts she has a headache, is not scared of it and realizes she just needs to take some painkillers and have an early night. In the second example, the physical sensation of a headache triggers anxious thoughts. These thoughts in turn trigger the body's alarm system, releasing adrenalin and causing more physical and psychological sensations. These additional sensations confirm to the person that there is something wrong with her and something awful is about to happen.

Some triggers for panic attacks

Anxiety and panic attacks start with a trigger. These triggers are not always obvious and can be very subtle. The most common triggers are:

- **A physical sensation** – this can be any pain or twinge in the body, or a change in breathing or heart rate caused by physical exertion. Other physical changes may include illness, tiredness, hunger, PMT or the effects of stimulants or drugs such as caffeine or alcohol.
- **Emotional distress**, such as grief, anger, sadness, frustration – for example, after an argument with a loved one.
- **Being alone or unoccupied**, which means you have more time to think about your panic attacks.
- **A thought or image flashing through your head** – for example, you might think 'What if I have a panic attack now?' or see yourself passed out on the floor. These thoughts and images can literally flash through your mind so quickly that you're not fully conscious of them.
- **Anticipatory anxiety** – for example, thoughts such as 'This is where I had a panic attack before, it's going to happen again.'
- **Hypervigilance or scanning** – as we saw in Chapter 3, when we experience frequent panic attacks and periods of high anxiety our body can become sensitized. This means that we become experts in scanning for any small change in our body or any physical sensation. These sensations would normally not be noticed or ignored by most people but because we are sensitized every small sensation seems important and triggers off our body's panic system. It is only natural that if you have been worrying a lot about your health or body, you will start to subconsciously look more closely for changes and be alert to any new sensation. We also tend to notice things more when they are important to us. If you have ever been expecting a baby, it may suddenly feel like the whole world is full of babies and you see reminders of this everywhere.
- **Environmental factors** – loud noises, hot environments and lighting can sometimes affect our senses and cause a physical sensa-tion which goes on to trigger a panic attack. For example, in a busy supermarket, there may be a lot of background noise and fluores-cent lighting, which could overload an already sensitized body's senses. Some experts believe that agoraphobics are more sensitive

to this environmental 'overload'; one study has shown that fluorescent lightning triggers symptoms in people with agoraphobia by increasing their heart rate.[15]

Try to discover what triggers your anxiety when you leave your home or 'safe zone'. Is it anticipatory anxiety? Do you think that because you've had a panic attack before in the shopping centre it is going to happen again? When you leave your safe zone, do you scan your body constantly and panic over any physical sensation? Is there an environmental trigger such as noise or lighting? Do you see images of yourself passed out or ill as you're walking along? It is important to try and analyse what is happening so that you're aware of the triggers and can prepare yourself to deal with them effectively by using alternative thoughts.

Look at this second example of how our perception of events can trigger a panic attack:

> You are walking down a road in the dark and you hear a noise. You think: 'There is someone following me, I'm going to be attacked.' Your heart starts to pound; you breathe more quickly and feel terribly afraid.

> You are walking down a road in the dark and you hear a noise. You think: 'Oh, it must be that cat I saw.' You turn around and see a cat running across the road. You continue walking.

In both examples, the trigger is hearing a noise, but two different thoughts produce different responses. In the first example, the trigger is interpreted in a catastrophic way – it assumes the worst possible scenario. These catastrophic thoughts send a message to your body that you're in danger and your body responds by getting ready to fight the danger or run away. Can you see that how we think is the key to whether a 'trigger' escalates into a full-blown panic attack?

When you're having a panic attack or feeling anxious, you can feel so swamped by your feelings and be so wiped out afterwards, that it can be hard to remember what the trigger was and what you were thinking at the time. To deal with this we need to find a way of capturing our thoughts and feelings before and during a panic attack.

Monitoring your triggers

The first step to controlling and managing these catastrophic thoughts is to be aware of your triggers and subsequent thoughts.

A thought diary

The best way of doing this is to keep a thought diary every day. Keep a record of the date, describe how you felt, the situation you were in and what your thoughts were. You also need a way of measuring how anxious you felt. This will prove useful when you progress to facing some of your feared situations. The easiest way of measuring your level of anxiety in a certain situation is to give it a score out of 10. Zero is feeling completely calm, 5 is feeling quite anxious and 10 is complete panic.

Here's an example of an entry in a thought diary:

Date: Saturday 15 July
Feelings – Very anxious, thought I was going to have a full-blown panic attack. 8 out of 10 on anxiety scale.
Situation – Queuing in a shop.
Thoughts – I kept thinking, what if I have a panic attack when I get to the till, I can't run away as everyone will think I'm mad. My legs feel shaky, what if I pass out? What if someone notices how panicky I feel, they will think I'm strange. I want to be somewhere safe; I just want to get out of here.

The aim of this exercise is to spot your automatic thoughts. An automatic thought is something which is so ingrained in you that you're not normally aware of it. Sometimes it is words or sometimes a picture will flash through your head. In the example, maybe the person could have seen a picture of herself passed out on the floor or an image of everyone looking at her strangely. This exercise is designed to help you analyse exactly what is happening in the build-up to a panic attack.

To capture these automatic thoughts, it is best to write down how you feel as soon as you start feeling anxious. However, it isn't always possible or practical to start writing in a notebook straight away. If that is the case, write down how you felt as soon as you can – perhaps carry a small notebook and pen in your bag. You do not only have to record panic attacks or episodes of high anxiety. As soon as you start to feel apprehensive, you can start writing. Write exactly how you feel, write down all the thoughts and images which are coming into your head. Don't think about what you are writing or about making sense, just let it all come out on paper. Some people find this process alone very therapeutic and calming.

If you start to feel anxious, use this as a sign to begin writing. Once you are calm again, it may be difficult to recall exactly what you were thinking. When keeping the diary, make sure the situation you were in is fully described. Had you had an argument with someone that day? Were you running late and rushing around? Did you have a deadline to meet? Were you worrying about somebody else? Were you feeling annoyed, angry or frustrated about something? Sometimes people spot a link between certain emotions and panic attacks. For example, they may find that a panic attack will occur after an argument; or if you feel frustrated because you have not been assertive enough in a certain situation, you may find that your repressed feelings of frustration come out as a panic attack.

It can be hard to capture your 'automatic' thoughts. They may be so ingrained that you're not fully aware of them, or they may flash through your mind so quickly that you don't notice them. Even if this is the case, it's worth persevering with your diary. Try to write things down while you are anxious or very soon afterwards. With practice, your ingrained thoughts should start to emerge. Like any new skill it takes time and practice before you start to see results. Make a note of anything you think or see, no matter how bizarre or weird it seems.

Once you have been keeping a diary for a couple of weeks, you should start to see some patterns or some common themes:

- Do your panic attacks happen at certain times? When you're tired or hungry? After an argument?
- Do similar thoughts and fears run through your mind each time? Are you worried about dying or feeling humiliated in public? Or afraid of going mad?

You may find it hard to believe that thoughts alone can create such strong feelings. This doesn't mean your feelings are 'all in your mind'. As we have seen, a panic attack produces very real physical symptoms, but the body is being tricked into triggering the fight or flight response when there is no danger to our survival. And it is our anxious thoughts which are tricking our body and triggering this response. Think of other situations where the mind can trick the body – when we watch a scary movie for example. Our heart thuds and beats faster even though we are in no physical danger. The body relies on our mind and thoughts to perceive when there is a danger and when to trigger its emergency response.

This is why our thoughts are so powerful and why it is important to manage your thoughts to overcome agoraphobia. The first step is to gain an awareness of your thoughts. Only then can you move on to managing and controlling them.

Controlling and managing your thoughts

There are various tools for controlling your thoughts. The rest of this chapter explores how to use the following tools:

- distraction;
- questioning your thoughts and beliefs;
- finding and using alternative thoughts.

Distraction

Distraction can be an effective tool to prevent anxiety from developing into a panic attack. Once you are experiencing a high level of anxiety it can be hard to challenge your thoughts. In the throes of anxiety, you need relief from your fears and this is where distraction can be useful. The aim of distraction, as the name suggests, is to distract you from your anxiety by focusing on something else. When you are distracted, you stop thinking anxious thoughts. This enables your stress response to slow down, helping you to become calm again.

For distraction to work, its focus has to demand all of your attention so you can't keep thinking about your anxiety. Distraction is a skill which needs to be learnt and becomes easier, and more effective, with practice.

You need to give some thought to what would work as a distraction tool for you. It should be something that is easy to do, demands a lot of attention and which you are interested in. There is no point choosing something you find completely dull, as it won't hold your attention and you'll quickly go back to worrying.

You could choose a physical exercise or a mental exercise, or focus closely on the things, people or objects around you. Examples of distraction include:

- going for a walk;
- playing a sport, if this is practical, or doing an exercise video at home;
- doing a physical task, such as washing up, cleaning, hoovering, handing out drinks at a party, reorganizing a room in your house;
- playing a computer game – there are many portable computer console devices available now and most mobile phones include games;
- doing a puzzle such as Sudoku, a crossword or a jigsaw;
- knitting;
- reading;
- listening to your favourite song or music;

- counting the number of people with blonde hair, or the number of red cars;
- imagining your favourite place – be it a hot beach, a ski slope or a pretty garden;
- if at work, squeezing a stress ball or attaching paper clips together;
- recalling mental arithmetic in your head – times tables, for example;
- reciting a song or poem in your head;
- closely observing everything you see around you.

Think about which form of distraction would suit you best, and try to come up with a couple of different distractions for different situations. Think of some common situations that make you anxious and work out which distraction would be the most effective in those situations. You will also need to rehearse the distraction; it's unlikely to work if you try it for the first time during a panic attack. So when you are feeling calm, try out the distraction technique. If it doesn't occupy you or hold your attention, keep trying until you find a method which does.

Care needs to be taken with distraction techniques. Although they are useful, you need to be sure that they're not being used to avoid a fear. For example, if you have a social anxiety about talking to guests at a party and you spend all your time in the kitchen, preparing food, cleaning and clearing up, these physical distraction activities are actually stopping you from facing your fear. So the distraction techniques become another part of your avoidance.

Distraction sometimes doesn't work if you haven't practised the technique enough, or if your anxiety levels are so high that you can't concentrate on the distraction. It is best to use distraction techniques as soon as you feel anxiety building, so that your anxiety does not escalate into a panic attack.

But distraction is just one tool. To truly overcome your agoraphobia you will need to start challenging your own thoughts and beliefs.

Questioning thoughts and beliefs

If you are keeping a daily thought diary, some of your most frequent and common thoughts should be emerging. Anxious thoughts tend to be catastrophic – they seem to assume the worst possible scenario in any given situation.

What you need to do next is to consider what the evidence is to support these thoughts. To begin with, it's best to do this exercise when you are feeling calm. Review your diary entries and pick out some thoughts to challenge. Ask yourself:

- What is the evidence to back this up? What is the evidence against it?
- If a friend told me this, what would I say to them?
- What is the likelihood of this happening?
- Has this ever happened before?
- Is there another way of looking at this?

Some examples of how you might tackle this are as follows:

Thought: I'm getting another headache, it must be a brain tumour.

Testing the thought: I have seen my doctor in the past and he has said my headaches were not a sign of a brain tumour or any illness, but are caused by anxiety. He is a qualified medical practitioner and I'm not. Feeling anxious causes tension headaches. Headaches are very common and brain tumours are very rare. The evidence suggests that it is highly unlikely I have a brain tumour and very likely that my headache is caused by tension.

Thought: I can't catch my breath – in a minute I'm going to stop breathing.

Testing the thought: My body can breathe automatically without my control. My body breathes perfectly well every night while I'm sleeping. When I get anxious, my body starts to hyperventilate to get extra oxygen for the muscles. Therefore, it is hyperventilation that is making me feel that I can't catch my breath.

Thought: I feel so scared that I'm going to pass out.

Testing the thought: It is almost impossible to faint while I'm feeling anxious. Fainting is caused by a drop in blood pressure which causes a reduction in the blood supply to the brain. When I'm anxious or having a panic attack my heart is beating faster and pumping more blood around my body. This means my blood pressure is getting higher, not lower, which it would need to do to cause me to faint.

Thought: Everyone can tell I'm anxious, they will think I'm weird.

Testing the thought: What evidence do I have to support this? Has anyone actually said I look anxious? Do I know what everyone around me is thinking? How can they tell what I'm thinking? Why is it weird to be anxious? Would I think somebody was weird for being nervous or having a phobia?

As these examples show, questioning your thoughts is all about exploring what the facts are and whether they support your beliefs. Are you jumping to conclusions based on little or no evidence? Could you convince a friend that what you think is real, let alone a court of law?

This process is designed to stop us from believing everything we think. Just because we think something does not make it real. It is about taking control by managing our thoughts. Even though thoughts can be ingrained and automatic, we can gain awareness of them, challenge them and replace them with more positive and helpful thoughts.

Finding and using alternative thoughts

The next step is to start replacing unhelpful thoughts with more accurate ones. In your thought diary, start to highlight all your automatic or anxious thoughts. How could you replace these thoughts with ones that are more positive?

One thought pattern that is very common during anxiety is the 'what ifs'. As we have seen earlier in this chapter, there is an initial trigger for anxiety or a panic attack. This trigger can be interpreted in different ways and your subsequent thoughts will decide whether or not your body sets off the fight or flight response. Common thoughts after this initial trigger can often start with 'what if'. For example, 'What if this is something serious?', 'What if somebody sees I'm having a panic attack?', 'What if this is the start of another panic attack?', 'What if I'm dying?', 'What if I'm having a heart attack?'

By having such thoughts you are adding fear to the initial anxiety, just like adding fuel to a fire which is only going to make the fire burn more strongly.

There are some important things to remember when you are experiencing panic attacks. Try reciting these sentences over and over, repeating them to yourself when you start to feel anxious. You may want to write them down on handy cards to look at whenever you feel anxious:

- A panic attack is not dangerous. These feelings are normal bodily reactions to stress.
- No one has ever died or suffered a serious mental illness from having a panic attack.
- I will not let normal bodily reactions stop me from going out.
- The danger is in my mind, not at . . . (wherever it is you want to go).
- This fear will pass if I let it and do not add frightening thoughts.
- Panic always subsides and I will feel calmer soon.

Red for stop

If you start to notice negative and anxious thoughts, immediately imagine a red traffic light for stop. Try to halt your thoughts and introduce positive thoughts to replace your negative ones. For example:

- Change 'I can't cope' to 'I can cope and I'm going to start by using my breathing exercise.'
- Change 'I have to do this' to 'I choose to do this and I want to do it.'
- Change 'I can't get nervous, I have to stay calm' to 'It's OK to feel a little nervous. But my fear will soon fade away as I keep relaxing.'
- Change 'I don't know how I got through being in that shop' to 'I've done really well in that shop, next time it's going to be even easier.'
- Change 'Let's get this over with as quickly as possible so I can get out' to 'I'm going to slow down and take my time. I will feel calmer soon.'

Sometimes you can challenge your thoughts with a question. So 'What if I get a panic attack?' becomes 'What if I don't have a panic attack? I have been out of my house plenty of times without panicking.'

The key is to be positive and kind to yourself, but without putting added pressure on yourself. Instead of thinking you 'must do' or 'have to do' something, try to think that you would 'like to do' and 'choose to do' it. You need to start regaining your confidence and control. Like many people with agoraphobia, you may feel as if you are no longer in control – you are at the mercy of your panic attacks, which could happen at any time.

But now is the time to take your control back. You do control your life and if you want to go out you can. With practice, you can control your panic attacks and help your body calm down. You are in control, not your anxiety, and the way you think and talk to yourself is the key to getting this control back.

Look again at the thoughts and fears you have written down in your thought diary. Are they as frightening when you see them on paper? Often these fears lose their potency once they've been written down. Looking at them when you are feeling calmer, do they seem realistic? Are they likely to be realized?

Positive images

Sometimes it isn't a thought which is frightening but an image. In this case, you will need to replace the image with something else. If you see yourself in a frightening situation, you can replace this image with another one of yourself in an enjoyable situation – perhaps lying on a warm beach or in a boat, or sitting in a beautiful field or on a hilltop.

Facing the worst

Once you are able to use alternative thoughts you may be ready to face the question: What is the worst that could happen? When we feel anxious, often the fear is lurking in the background, a vague sense that something terrible will happen. When we are aware of what the worst is, we can start to face this fear. Often, the worst scenario is not as fearful as it seems.

For example, you might be walking along the road and be gripped by fear of passing out. In this case, the worst thing that could happen is that you actually faint. As we've already seen, the likelihood of fainting during a panic attack is almost nil. However, if you did actually pass out, would that be so bad? Someone would help you. Your body would correct the shortage of oxygen in your brain and passing out would not cause you any serious damage.

For many, the ultimate fear of a panic attack is that you are going to die. Fears of death can be difficult to deal with. It is important to remind yourself that no one has died from a panic attack. Even if it's hard to believe that such strong physical sensations could be caused by a stress reaction, your physical symptoms are the symptoms of the stress response and not of any other illness, as your doctor has confirmed.

Further help

The Further Reading section at the back of this book gives details of books that can help you to manage your thoughts. However, changing your thoughts on your own can be difficult. While some people are successful with a self-help programme, others need more support. If you find it difficult to recognize and challenge negative thoughts on your own, you may need to consider seeing a therapist if you are not already doing so. The next chapter explores how to find the right psychological therapy for you. Keeping a thought diary will still be very worthwhile and will probably be one of the tasks your therapist sets you. You could also try talking to an understanding friend or family member. Tell her about some of your negative or anxious thoughts. Ask her whether she thinks they are realistic and what she would tell herself instead.

It takes time, but once you start to spot your triggers, you have found a big piece of the jigsaw. There is an explanation for your panic attacks. Once you start to uncover these triggers, you're not only learning more about yourself but also taking a big leap forward in the effort to finally conquer your fears.

9

Psychological treatments

You may have exhausted all your self-help techniques and still feel you aren't making any progress. Or you may find it hard to motivate yourself and, despite your best intentions, find it difficult to make changes by yourself.

Some people find self-help really useful, and feel more comfortable because they are in control. Other people find they need the support of someone else. You might find it helps to talk to someone who does not judge you or criticize you. Having a regular appointment with someone each week may also motivate you to carry out your relaxation exercises and any other tasks you have been set – whereas you may put off doing them if you are left to your own devices.

If you have been agoraphobic for a very long time or your agoraphobia is very severe, you may see no way out. You may find it hard to imagine how you will ever get over it. You may not feel you have the strength to tackle it alone and need the moral and emotional support that a therapist can give. A therapist can guide you through a treatment, breaking it down into small and manageable chunks.

Psychological therapies are known as 'talking therapies'. There are various types, and each type takes a different approach to tackling a problem. There is evidence that some are better than others at treating anxiety and agoraphobia. However, each case of agoraphobia is different. It's important to find the right method, and the right therapist, for you.

You may not want to take medication or you may feel that medication alone is not enough to get to the root cause of your problem. Psychological therapies have been shown to be very effective in the treatment of many mental health problems, including agoraphobia.

You can be referred for treatment by your GP; however, not all the psychotherapies listed here will be available in your NHS trust. There can also be long waiting lists. Another option would be to see a therapist privately. Some private therapists offer lower fees for the unwaged, so it's worth checking this with them. It is important to make sure your therapist has a recognized qualification; your GP can help you establish this. If you're finding a private therapist, contact an accredited organization (see Useful addresses for details).

Research has shown that the effectiveness of any therapy depends on a good relationship between the therapist and client. This doesn't mean you need to be close friends, but you both need a commitment to the therapy and you should have a good working relationship. If this is not the case, then you may need to consider a different therapist.

You may wonder how many sessions will be needed. There are no set guidelines, although if you are receiving treatment on the NHS you may be given a fixed number of sessions. NICE guidelines recommend between 7 and 14 hours, delivered within four months.[16] Because agoraphobia is a complex phobia, it is likely that you will need the maximum number of sessions.

Deciding to have therapy can be a big step. If you've waited a long time, you may simply feel relieved and grateful to get the therapy. Or you may feel a little uneasy. When you walk into the therapist's room it can be upsetting to feel that you do have a problem which needs help. You might wonder what other people will think, or you may feel there is a stigma attached to having psychological therapy. You may even feel a little ashamed that it has come to this.

It is perfectly normal to have mixed feelings about going into therapy. You may come away from your first couple of sessions disappointed. You may have thought that the therapist could come up with some cure and you'd feel better immediately. When you realize that it is you who has to do the hard work, you who has to face your fears, and that the therapist is there simply to guide you, it can be a little disheartening.

Despite all these concerns, therapy has been very effective for large numbers of people. It is a big step and for it to work you really need to want to change. You also need to be prepared to start facing your fears. Of course, you won't be thrown in the deep end, but you need to be prepared to start facing situations that you may have been avoiding for a long time. It is unlikely that a psychotherapist will visit you at home. So for agoraphobics who are severely housebound, just getting to see the therapist represents a big step.

At times, therapy can be emotional; it can also be very rewarding. You may be talking about feelings you've kept buried for some time. Dealing with and facing your fears can be hard, but for many agoraphobics, therapy represents the turning point in their lives.

Many different approaches are used by therapists, and the main types are outlined in the rest of this chapter. If there is any evidence that a therapy is effective for anxiety disorders, then this is also stated. This should give you the information you need to decide which type of therapy is right for you. You can then discuss this with your GP, or book a private session.

Types of therapist

- **Psychologist.** A general term for someone who has studied psychology, normally at degree level. There are different branches of psychology, including criminal and educational psychology. A clinical psychologist is someone who has undertaken further training in order to be able to treat patients with emotional or behavioural problems.
- **Psychiatrist.** A psychiatrist is a medical doctor who has gone on to specialize in mental illness and disorders. Only psychiatrists and medical doctors can prescribe medications.
- **Counsellor/psychotherapist.** There is very little difference between these two terms. A psychotherapist or counsellor who is a member of the UK Council for Psychotherapy will have undertaken four-year, postgraduate training on working with people with emotional and mental difficulties. If you are seeing a counsellor or psychotherapist privately then it is best to choose one from a recognized organization (see Useful addresses).

Types of therapy

A therapist will normally specialize in one, or sometimes more than one, approach to psychotherapy. There are many different approaches to psychotherapy but the following is a brief overview of the main types.

Applied relaxation therapy

Applied relaxation therapy is also known as relaxation training. A therapist will work with you to teach you how to relax. You will be taught specific exercises on how to relax the muscles in your body and how to relax your body in stressful situations. You will need to practise the exercises at home. Research shows that when the body relaxes, the mind also seems to calm down.[17] Applied relaxation therapy has been shown to be effective for treating anxiety disorders. Research indicates that it can be as effective as cognitive behavioural therapy.[18] An exercise to relax the muscles of your body is provided in Chapter 7.

Behavioural therapy

This form of therapy aims to change patterns of behaviour. The approach takes the view that although behaviour is learnt in response to past experiences, these experiences do not need to be analysed in order to change our behaviour – in the case of people with agoraphobia, the behaviour of not leaving your home or 'safety' zone. Behavioural therapy is sometimes also called exposure therapy. It works on reintroducing someone to the situation she fears and getting her to remain in that situation until she no longer feels afraid of it. You will learn ways of managing your anxiety levels and may be asked to keep a diary or practise new skills in between sessions.

For agoraphobia, you would normally identify a list of situations you fear, ranging from those which worry you the least to the most. Then your therapist would encourage you to gradually work through this list. Until you had learnt to be completely comfortable in one current situation, you wouldn't progress to the next situation. This form of therapy has been shown to be particularly effective in treating anxiety disorders, phobias and obsessive-compulsive disorders. Chapter 10 guides you through a behavioural therapy exercise you can use to tackle your agoraphobia.

Counselling

Counselling tends to work on a less intense level than psychotherapy. The British Psychological Society defines counselling as a system intended to 'help people improve their sense of wellbeing, alleviate their distress, resolve their crises and increase their ability to solve problems and make decisions for themselves'. This suggests that it works best for people who need help through a specific crisis and may be less useful for a more complex problem such as agoraphobia, especially if you have been suffering from the condition for a long time. That is not to say that it does not offer any benefit, but other forms of therapy have been shown to be more effective for treating agoraphobia.

Cognitive behaviour therapy (CBT)

Cognitive behaviour therapy shares a lot of similarities with behaviour therapy, as it focuses on changing the present and future rather than on the past. While behaviour therapy looks at directly changing our behaviour, CBT aims to change our thinking patterns as well as our behaviour. It explores how we think and helps us to get rid of negative and unhelpful ways of thinking. CBT remains the number one treatment for anxiety disorders, as well as for other disorders such as depression and eating disorders. NICE guidelines recommend cognitive behavioural therapy for panic disorder with agoraphobia. There is also substantial evidence to support the effectiveness of CBT in treating anxiety disorders.

If you are referred for NHS treatment, it is very likely that you will be offered a course of CBT. The number of sessions offered and waiting times will vary across the country but the government is increasing investment in CBT in order to cut waiting times and address the shortage of therapists.[19] CBT is not a 'passive' therapy – you will not spend all your time talking about your feelings. You will be challenged to face your fears and will be taken out of your comfort zone with the support of your therapist.

Computerized cognitive behaviour therapy (CCBT)

Currently, the demand for CBT outstrips the number of available therapists. To address this shortfall, the government is introducing computerized self-help programmes. The programmes can be accessed via any computer with an internet connection. The advantage of these programmes is that they can be accessed instantly, cutting out the long wait for therapy. In addition, for agoraphobics it means that you can get help at home rather than facing the difficulties of going to a therapist.

NICE recommends the use of a programme called FearFighter for agoraphobia, as well as for other panic disorders and phobias. FearFighter has been tested in clinical trials and has proven to be an effective therapy.[20] Your GP simply prescribes you access to FearFighter and arranges for you to be sent a password to use the site. You also have telephone support. At the time of writing, PCTs were in the process of implementing these programmes and there is a legal duty for PCTs to make a treatment approved by NICE available. You can also buy the programme privately, at a cost of £350.

Experiential therapy

This approach is based on the assumption that we build our individual picture of the world from our experiences, and that what we do, believe and feel is largely dictated by the model of the world we create. The first task in this type of therapy is to identify how someone sees the world; he or she will then be helped to construct a different view of the world. The therapy often has a specific focus and it has an emphasis on 'doing'. It aims to introduce positive changes in the short term as well as dealing with the underlying issues over the long term. Experiential therapy may be useful for people who find 'talking' therapies difficult and who may feel more comfortable with drama, art, dance or animal-assisted therapies. This form of therapy can be a good choice for children and adolescents.

Hypnotherapy

This refers to any therapy in which hypnosis is used as the main approach. Hypnosis can be described as a state of deep relaxation in which a person is neither asleep nor awake. In this state, he is more receptive and will be given therapeutic suggestions by the therapist in order to change his behaviour or relieve his symptoms. The therapy is designed to tackle deep-seated problems and habits by working with the unconscious mind. For example, someone who is having panic attacks may be told that he will no longer be frightened by them. Hypnosis is also sometimes used in psychotherapy to remove barriers that the conscious mind might otherwise create to prevent full psychological exploration.

There is some evidence from clinical trials that hypnosis can be effective for anxiety disorders and phobias.[21] Evidence also suggests that hypnosis can enhance the effects of cognitive behavioural therapy for anxiety and phobias.[22]

It is important that you see a trained, experienced and regulated hypnotherapist. At the moment, there is no one single regulatory body for hypnotherapists. However, anyone using hypnosis as a psychotherapeutic tool should be registered with the British Psychological Society, the British Association for Counselling and Psychotherapy or with a member organization of the United Kingdom Council for Psychotherapy. Contact details of these organizations are given in Useful addresses.

Integrative therapy

This means the therapist uses more than one approach in a formal integration. For example, a therapist may use a combination of humanistic and psychodynamic approaches (see below).

Humanistic psychotherapy

This type of therapy encourages people to explore their feelings and take responsibility for their thoughts and actions. It tries to deal with the whole person: mind, body and spirit. The emphasis is on self-development and the therapy is 'client-centred'. The client's creative instincts may be used to explore and resolve personal issues.

Person-centred therapy

Sometimes known as 'Rogerian' after Carl Rogers, who developed the method, this approach aims to help the client to see herself as a person and to empower her to make changes. The therapist allows the person to freely express her emotions without making any judgement, so as to allow her to deal with her negative feelings. The therapist does not suggest how the client should change, but instead listens and mirrors back to her what he has heard, so she can work out what she needs to do to overcome her difficulties.

Psychoanalysis

This approach is based on the work of Sigmund Freud. He believed that unacceptable thoughts in early childhood are banished to the unconscious mind but continue to influence thoughts, emotions and behaviour, and that these repressed feelings can surface later as conflicts or depression, or through dreams. In this approach, the therapist seeks to interpret these repressed feelings from our past and make them acceptable to the client's conscious mind. 'Transference', where feelings about figures in the client's life are transferred to the therapist, is encouraged. This type of therapy can be a lengthy and intensive process.

Psychodynamic therapy

Like psychoanalysis, psychodynamic therapy focuses on discussing past experiences and how they might have led to the current situation. It also explores our feelings towards people close to us. It is believed that this understanding frees us to make choices about what happens in the future. For specific difficulties a brief course of psychodynamic psychotherapy may be all that is needed. For problems that have been experienced for a long time, then regular sessions may be needed for many months. The psychodynamic approach is derived from psychoanalysis but is believed to provide a quicker solution to emotional problems.

Systemic therapies

A term often used to describe group therapies, such as family or marital therapy. People are sometimes seen individually but the focus in a systemic approach is on their relationships with others. The therapy normally aims to promote a change in how the members of a group interact with each other and in the dynamics of relationships. Unless your agoraphobia is closely linked to a relationship difficulty, then you may feel that another therapy would be more suitable.

Transpersonal therapy

This describes any form of counselling or therapy which assumes a spiritual dimension to life and nature. It also assumes that all beings with a higher spiritual power are connected and that whatever hardships we go through, our spirits are undamaged. Transpersonal therapy focuses on personal development. It looks at the issues in our past but also at how we can face the challenges of the future.

Choosing a therapy

You might be wondering how to choose between these various types of therapy. Your choice may well depend on whether you are receiving NHS treatment or whether you can afford to see a therapist privately. If you are receiving help on the NHS then you may be offered counselling (there tend to be shorter waiting lists for this) or cognitive behavioural therapy. Unless the counsellor has been trained in CBT techniques then it is advisable to ask your GP to refer you for CBT instead.

If you are going to see a therapist privately, then I would recommend that you try CBT or behavioural therapy initially as according to the evidence they are most effective in treating anxiety disorders. If you find that CBT is not effective for you and you feel that you have issues stemming from childhood or past experiences, then it may be worth seeing a different type of therapist. You may feel that you need to deal with these deeper issues before you can attempt to change your behaviour. Other people find CBT effective and do not need, or wish, to explore their past.

Hypnosis may also be another useful therapy, either on its own or alongside CBT. Another advantage of CBT and hypnosis is that both methods try to produce changes in behaviour quickly, i.e. within four months, whereas other forms of therapy may take much longer. If you are suffering from an anxiety disorder or have been housebound for a long time, then you will most likely be very eager to see some positive changes quickly.

With the right therapist, there is every reason to be positive and many people have overcome agoraphobia with psychotherapy. Therapy is not easy, because it means we have to face situations we've been avoiding for a long time. But making the commitment to start therapy is a big leap on to the path to recovery.

10

Stepping out

Each person's agoraphobia will affect him or her in different ways. But we all have our own 'safe zone' or safe place and when we try to go outside this, our anxieties kick in. Your safe zone may stretch no further than your home, or you may be able to visit some places and not others; maybe you can go out locally but not to the busy town centre. Or you may be able to travel but only on certain conditions; perhaps you can only go by car, or with someone you trust.

As this book has shown, there are many different therapies and techniques you can use to reduce your anxiety and prepare you for tackling your agoraphobia. But no matter which methods or treatments you choose, there is no escaping the fact that if you want to overcome your agoraphobia you will need to start facing the situations you have been avoiding.

You may only have been avoiding these situations for weeks or you may have had your agoraphobia for many years. It doesn't matter how long you have been agoraphobic – the way to treat it is the same. Of course, if you have been housebound for several years it isn't realistic to expect to be waltzing round the supermarket in a week. But it is possible to overcome agoraphobia, no matter how long you have had the condition.

Self-exposure

The technique outlined in this chapter is called self-exposure, also sometimes referred to as graded practice or behavioural therapy. This technique has been proven to be effective in treating phobias, including agoraphobia. Most cognitive behavioural therapists will use self-exposure techniques.

As the name suggests, self-exposure means exposing yourself to the situations or places you fear. This is a gradual process and the aim is to get you so used to a place or situation that you stop being afraid of it.

You may be sceptical whether this will work, but we have already seen how avoiding a fear makes that fear stronger. By avoiding, say, supermarkets and shopping centres, you are reinforcing to your mind and body that these places are dangerous and that the fight or flight response should be triggered if you end up there. Of course, we know rationally that our survival is not being threatened by a trip to the supermarket, but our body will respond automatically, just as it should, to our mind's anxious thoughts. By starting to go into these situations again, and remaining there until we feel calm, we are teaching our mind and body that this situation is safe and there is no need for the fight or flight response to be triggered.

Self-exposure is not always easy, and you will have good days and bad days. If you asked most people to start facing their innermost fears, they would find it very difficult. But if you stick at it then it has been shown to be effective in treating agoraphobia. To increase your chances of success, make sure you have made any changes to your lifestyle that may have been increasing your anxiety. It's also very useful to be familiar with your breathing and relaxation exercises and to be aware of your anxious thoughts. Trying to replace them with positive thoughts will also help you.

Of course, if you are carrying out these lifestyle changes and exercises within the safety of your home, then it's likely you'll be feeling fine. In fact, you may not have been feeling anxious at all, because your avoidance has cut out all the situations which cause you to panic. You may not have thought the relaxation and breathing exercises were needed because you have not been feeling anxious. But when it comes to tackling agoraphobia by stepping out, we need as many tools as possible to help us. The most helpful tools will be distraction techniques, breathing and relaxation exercises and thought control. It is important to keep practising these techniques so you are familiar with them, because once you start feeling nervous it can be hard to remember things.

As mentioned before, self-exposure is a gradual process. You can literally take it one step at a time. You do need to be prepared to leave your comfort zone and experience some fear, but by no means will you be thrust into the deep end without warning. You will be in control of the process.

Rules for self-exposure

There are a few ground rules when carrying out self-exposure to make sure it will help you overcome agoraphobia in the long term.

- **Go slowly.** The aim is to stay in the situation calmly. Do not rush it so that the whole experience is over as quickly as possible, for example running down the road instead of walking so you can return home more quickly. Stay in the situation until any panic passes – it will pass if you let it. Leave the situation only when you feel calm and in control of your anxieties. It is natural that you will feel anxious to begin with, but use this as an opportunity to try out your techniques of distraction and replace any negative thoughts with positive ones. Relax any tense muscles and breathe slowly and deeply from your stomach. It is better to walk down one street feeling calm than to get inside a supermarket and rush round in an anxious manner trying to get out as quickly as possible.

- **Be alone.** Don't take a friend or carer with you – the aim is to be able to face your feared situations alone, without relying on someone else. If you have been used to going everywhere with a carer, then think carefully about what your first ten situations should be.
- **Don't progress too quickly.** After a couple of successes it's easy to get ambitious and think 'Right, tomorrow I'm going to tackle number 10 on my list!' Take your time and don't see your list as a race.
- **Keep records.** It's important to keep diary records so you can measure your progress. It may not feel as if you are making any progress, but when you look back at your diary entries you will see that actually you are progressing.

Starting your self-exposure programme

You're now ready to start your programme of self-exposure. Your first task is to draw up a list of ten situations or places you would like to be able to visit. Be realistic and make each situation a little more challenging than the last. This list will very much depend on your agoraphobia, where you live and whether you are completely housebound or able to travel to some places. So, for someone housebound living in a fairly built-up area, their list might look like this:

1 Walk to the bottom of my road and back.
2 Walk to the bottom of the next road and back.
3 Walk to my nearest small shop (such as a newsagent), look in the window, and walk back.
4 Walk to my nearest small shop, go inside and look around at the items and walk back.
5 Walk to my nearest small shop, go inside and buy one item and walk back.
6 Visit a bigger or busier shop. Go inside, look at some items and then go home.

7 Visit a bigger or busier shop. Go inside, buy a couple of items and then go home.

8 Walk into a supermarket and look at the magazines or items near the entrance. Without buying anything, walk past the tills, then exit and go home.

9 Walk into a supermarket, walk down two aisles and then exit and go home.

10 Walk into a supermarket, walk down first two aisles, buy one item at the tills and then go home.

Can you see how these steps gradually increase in difficulty but there isn't a huge leap between them? The first step is very reasonable – if you are severely housebound then simply stepping out of the front door for one minute could be your first step. If you were asked to attempt step 10 on the list as your first task then it could be overwhelming, but step 1 seems achievable. Only you will know what is achievable for your situation. However, remember that the aim is to extend your safety zone. You will need to stretch yourself by choosing situations which will challenge you – the key is not to pick a situation that will completely overwhelm you.

Keeping records

After you have drawn up your list, your second task will be to organize a record-keeping system. Before each practice, write down in a notepad the date, where you are going and how you are feeling. When you get back from carrying out your practice, write down how anxious you felt in the situation. You should grade your anxiety levels on a scale of 0 to 10 – where 0 is complete relaxation, 5 is fairly anxious and 10 is absolute panic. As well as grading your anxiety, write down how you felt while you were in the situation, what thoughts came into your head, how you dealt with them, what you felt went well and what you found challenging.

After going out, review what you found challenging and see if there are any strategies you might use to deal with these issues. For example, did you use your breathing and relaxation exercises – were they effective? Do you need to practise them more often? What thoughts came into your head – what would be a more positive thought? And now you are calmer, how could you challenge those thoughts? What could you say to yourself next time that would reassure you? Take a note of these positive, reassuring thoughts so you can remember to use them next time.

Building your self-exposure

Keep practising this same situation over and over again, every day if you can manage it. When you find you can handle the situation calmly and it is not causing you high levels of anxiety, progress to the next situation on your list. Another indication that you are ready to move on to the next stage is that your anxiety grade is lower than when you started out. If you started out grading a situation at 7 or 8 and now you grade it as 3 or 4 it is probably time to move on and challenge yourself a little more.

It may take a long time for you to feel absolutely no anxiety when you go out, but this shouldn't stop you from progressing with your list of chosen situations. What you are looking for is an improvement, the feeling that any fear you experience is under control. You may feel a little uneasy in a situation but you are in control, you are not on the verge of a panic attack – it may take a long time for you to actually 'enjoy' being out! When you are in control of a situation on a regular basis then it's time to move on. There is a balance to be struck between challenging yourself and throwing yourself in the deep end. You need to experience some anxiety in order to get better, but this anxiety should not overwhelm you.

There is a fine line between being realistic about your self-exposure and employing avoidance. Generally, when you start out on self-exposure you want to have as many positive experiences as possible. You want to build up your confidence and feel empowered to tackle new situations. For this reason, it may not be a good idea to practise when you are experiencing one of your triggers. For example, if you feel anxious when your blood sugar drops, make sure you have eaten before going out. If you normally feel more anxious when you are very tired, or have a headache or a cold, it may be better to leave your practice until the next day.

But make sure that you do not excuse yourself too easily. This is a form of avoidance! Having a headache or a cold, or feeling a bit tired, wouldn't stop most people from leaving the house, although they might well prefer to be at home. In this situation, it is better to go out still, but perhaps to scale down your outing. If you are on step 2 or 3 of your list then you may wish to try step 1 on a day when your anxiety levels are already high. If you are on step 1, then you may wish to do half of it. It is important that you don't invent new ways to avoid situations, but also that you build up your confidence.

Be kind to yourself, and give yourself lots of praise! Every time you move up a notch on your list, try to celebrate in some way. It's important to celebrate and recognize your success. It may not feel a huge achievement to do something your partner or family does every day, but it is a major achievement for you. Your family, friends and partner do not have a fear of leaving the house. Put them in a situation or with an object they fear above all else and you would probably find they wouldn't cope too well at first either! You are facing and conquering your fears every time you leave your house or safety zone – that deserves some recognition and praise.

Coping with setbacks

Not every day will be a good day. There will be some days when you sail through your exercise with no panic and others where you feel you cannot see the task through. This can be particularly difficult after previous successes and you may feel as if you have taken a step backwards.

Try not to get too disappointed or upset with yourself if you have a bad day. All of us have good days and bad days. It's helpful if you can stay in the situation until you feel calmer because this stops your mind reinforcing the feeling that the situation is dangerous. However, in reality it's likely that there will be occasions when this isn't possible. This doesn't mean you have gone back to square one – go home and write about what happened in your diary. Try to work out what happened. What triggered your panic in this situation? What thoughts were you thinking? How can you address them? You have to turn into a bit of a detective and hunt for the clues and triggers in a situation.

A fear of something unknown can feel overwhelming; once you can start to identify your fears and put them down on paper it is a lot easier to develop arguments to counteract them. Just as the bogeyman disappears in the daytime, so your fears will start to evaporate once you explore them in the cold light of day.

Look at every time you leave your safety zone as an opportunity to practise the relaxation techniques you've been rehearsing. The most important – and the hardest – thing to learn is acceptance. You need to accept that you have agoraphobia and that for the time being it is just part of who you are. Don't try to fight it, this is not a battle. It is about learning to relax, learning to accept and going with the flow. Take the good days with the bad, and persevere. There is always hope and no need to give up on overcoming agoraphobia. Overcoming setbacks and bad days is all part of the journey.

Sometimes a life event or another stress can trigger a setback that lasts more than just a couple of days. It could be that you have progressed high up your list and the setback means you can't face the same situations. In this case, start again at the bottom of your list and gradually work your way back up. You will not be losing out on anything. In fact, you will be gaining more and more experience in dealing with your agoraphobic symptoms, and this can only be helpful.

The next step

When you have finished your first ten situations, you can simply create a new list of ten more situations. Keep carrying on in this way until you are able to move around freely wherever you want. When you are practising visiting places close to your home, there is obviously less risk because you know you can get home quickly. The further away you travel, the longer the journey home, which can be off-putting. The way to tackle this is to gradually increase the range and distance of the places you visit. You should approach these new situations in exactly the same way.

You may reach the stage where you feel you don't need your list any more – fantastic! Don't hold yourself back. If you feel like going somewhere, then great, get out there! But if you do have a setback then simply go back to the list and work your way back up again. The ultimate aim of self-exposure is to teach yourself that this feeling of safety and calmness lives inside you, not in a building. The reason you feel safe at home is because you tell yourself you do and you truly believe that you are only safe there. Once you learn that you can keep this inner sense of peace within you, wherever you go, you have gone a long way to truly overcoming your agoraphobia.

Jill

Jill, 45, used self-exposure to overcome her agoraphobia.

> I'd been seeing a cognitive behavioural therapist for a few weeks when they suggested I should start facing situations I was afraid of. We drew up a list together of some situations I felt I might be able to go into. To be honest, at the time I didn't think I'd be able to do any of them. I was used to going everywhere with my husband, usually by car. So to actually go out by myself was very scary.
>
> My first task was to walk to a local shop about ten minutes away and buy a newspaper. The shop is small and there aren't normally any queues. The first few times were difficult. I didn't have a panic attack but it just felt so weird and strange. I felt quite off-balance and this sounds silly, but it felt strange to be walking. I felt quite agitated inside the shop and I couldn't wait to pay for the newspaper and dash out. I always felt calmer walking home, I started to speed up as I got nearer to my house. I was always

relieved to get back inside but after a while I'd be really happy that I'd actually done it.

To start off with I didn't think I was making much progress. Yes, I was going out, but I didn't enjoy it and certainly didn't linger! But my therapist pointed out that just getting out, buying the newspaper and walking home was a big achievement as I hadn't been doing this before. And after a couple of weeks, I did notice it was easier to do and started to slow down. It was part of my routine and didn't feel so strange.

My confidence started to build from there and I realized for the first time that I could get over this. Every few months, I would set myself new goals and it was a real thrill to achieve them. I'm lucky to have such a supportive husband. He really helped me and gave me positive encouragement if I had a bad day.

I think I'm definitely over the worst. I get anxious from time to time but I can't remember the last time I had a proper panic attack. I'm going on holiday abroad this year – it has been five years since I've had a holiday. I can't wait! My advice to other people with agoraphobia is to try and stay positive and keep at it, even after a bad day.

If you find it very hard to carry out a self-help programme then don't despair. It could be for many different reasons – it doesn't mean that your agoraphobia cannot be treated. It just means that you may be more suited to face-to-face therapy. The support of a therapist will give you the added help you need to tackle your agoraphobia.

Six steps to stepping out

1 Write down a list of ten situations you would like to face. Gradually increase the difficulty of each situation.
2 Keep a diary of your thoughts and feelings – write in it before and after you go out.
3 Record how anxious you felt when out on a scale of 0 to 10.
4 When you are out, stay in the situation until you feel calm. The feelings of panic will pass. They are not harmful, just your body's normal reactions to stress. Use all your relaxation techniques to help speed up the passing of panic.
5 Be aware of your mind's sneaky avoidance tactics. Regularly review your progress, celebrate success and make sure your list of situations is challenging enough without being overwhelming.
6 Accept your agoraphobia and accept that you will still feel symptoms of panic. Bad days and setbacks are all part of the journey.

11

Women's health and agoraphobia

The number of women with agoraphobia is much higher than the number of men. This could simply be down to men being more reluctant to report their symptoms. But it could also mean that women are more susceptible to agoraphobia.

Some academics think that women may be susceptible because of their traditional role of being 'at home'. Others think that female hormones may play a part, and anecdotal evidence does point towards a link between female hormones and anxiety levels.

There are certain times in a woman's life which are truly life-changing and might also have a big effect on your agoraphobic symptoms. Many of us will be very familiar with that ratty, irritable feeling each month before our period. You may be lucky enough never to get pre-menstrual tension (PMT), or pre-menstrual syndrome (PMS) as it's also known, but this doesn't mean your monthly cycle isn't affecting your agoraphobia.

It's helpful to have an understanding of how our sex hormones work and the role they play during pivotal times in your life: at puberty, during your monthly cycle, during pregnancy and birth, and in the menopause.

Hormones are chemicals that are made in several parts of the body. Some have an immediate effect, such as adrenalin – we have explored in detail the symptoms adrenalin causes. Others, such as growth and sex hormones, work more slowly.

During puberty, the pituitary gland (a small organ the size of a pea underneath your brain) releases hormones which prompt the sex organs to start producing sex hormones. In girls, the ovaries start making oestrogen and progesterone. These two hormones work together to control the menstrual cycle, and play a major part in other changes in a woman's life such as pregnancy, birth and the menopause.

The menstrual cycle

Some women go through their monthly cycle without noticing any changes. But I think it's fair to say that the majority of us are not so lucky. There are many physical symptoms of PMS such as back pain, headaches, stomach cramps, and painful or swollen breasts. None of these are pleasant but it's the mood changes that can really play havoc when we're trying to get over agoraphobia. We can suddenly feel much more tired than normal, irritable or weepy about things we wouldn't normally get upset about, and generally life can just get on top of us.

But what is happening inside our body each month to cause so many physical and emotional symptoms? During a typical monthly cycle, the pituitary gland releases a follicle-stimulating hormone which travels around the bloodstream and stimulates the ovaries to start ripening eggs. Some of the egg-containing sacs, called follicles, start to mature and one, occasionally two or more, grows faster than the others. The follicle-stimulating hormone also triggers the ovaries to produce oestrogen. Oestrogen helps the eggs to mature and starts thickening the lining of the uterus so that it is ready to accept the egg if fertilization occurs.

Ovulation occurs when the pituitary gland releases a surge both of a follicle-stimulating hormone and of another hormone called luteinizing hormone. These hormones cause the mature egg to leave the sac and move down the fallopian tube. Just before ovulation, oestrogen changes the secretions of your cervix to a clear, stretchy fluid, allowing sperm to swim through the cervix to fertilize the egg. After ovulation, the ovaries start to produce progesterone, which prepares the lining of the uterus by making it thick and spongy so that the egg can settle there. After ovulation, progesterone also causes the mucus from the cervix to become thick and sticky to stop sperm from passing through.

If the egg is fertilized in the fallopian tube, then it travels into the uterus and settles into the lining. It takes about five days for an egg to travel from the ovary to the uterus. If this happens your levels of oestrogen and progesterone will stay high and early symptoms of pregnancy will start to occur.

If the egg isn't fertilized or successfully implanted, then it starts to break away. Levels of oestrogen and progesterone drop and the lining of the uterus starts to produce prostaglandins. These chemicals break up the lining and stimulate the uterus to contract. Your period will then start and the lining of uterus and egg will be shed. The first day of your period is known as day one of your cycle. During your period the next batch of approximately 20 eggs will start to develop in the ovary. PMS normally starts some time after ovulation. PMS can last for the whole two weeks before a period starts and most women find that the symptoms disappear when their period begins. However, some women find that their symptoms do not go away until their period finishes.

Symptoms of PMS

So this explains the hormonal changes taking place, but it doesn't give us any answers as to how to deal with it. There is no scientific evidence as to the exact causes of PMS; a few experts may even suggest that it doesn't even exist. But I think most of us don't need any convincing that it's a very real problem. The general consensus is that it is the production of progesterone that causes the symptoms of PMS. You may be surprised to learn that over 150 symptoms of PMS have been identified. Some of these are physical and some are psychological. The most common symptoms include:

- breast soreness
- fluid retention and bloating
- headaches
- skin and hair changes
- depression, anxiety and agitation
- feeling irritable or experiencing mood swings
- stomach cramps

The number of symptoms and their severity varies from woman to woman and can also vary from month to month. So one month you may be symptom free and in another month be affected. Some women never experience PMS, while others find that the symptoms severely affect their lives. PMS often starts during a time of major hormonal change such as puberty, pregnancy, after having a baby or in the run-up to the menopause. PMS also tends to run in families.

Agoraphobia and PMS

If you suffer from agoraphobia it is worth seeing if your monthly cycle has any impact on your anxiety levels. Women with low levels of serotonin (which you may have if you are suffering from an anxiety disorder or depression) have been shown to be more sensitive to increased levels of progesterone. So having an anxiety disorder such as agoraphobia could make you more susceptible to PMS. So, if in the two weeks before your period you experience more anxiety and panic attacks, then this could be why.

Your PMS may cause you to feel more tense, more irritable and anxious. You might find that you seem to have more panic attacks around this time or that it's harder to get out and about. The only way to find out if it is having an effect is to keep a diary of your symptoms for two to three months. Monitor any symptoms throughout the monthly cycle, along with your anxiety levels. This will help you decide if hormones are playing a part in your agoraphobia. The

Natural Health Advisory Service, which treats symptoms of PMS, IBS and the menopause with nutritional changes, carried out a survey of 500 women with PMS in 2007. The survey found that 94 per cent of the sample experienced anxiety before a period and 36 per cent experienced agoraphobia. So it's really worth seeing if your hormones are playing a part in your anxiety.

Treatment for PMS

It's a good idea to discuss your symptoms with your doctor, as there are various treatment options. Showing your doctor your diaries will also help as you will have some clear evidence to back up what you are saying. There are generally three different ways of tackling PMS:

- **Hormonal therapy.** The aim of these treatments is to prevent ovulation, stopping the usual monthly increase in progesterone. However, each hormonal treatment may have some drawbacks. The combined oral contraceptive pill is sometimes prescribed but as this contains progesterone some symptoms of PMS can persist. Or the contraceptive injection may be prescribed, but in some cases this can worsen symptoms of PMS. A synthetic steroid can also be prescribed, but it needs to be monitored carefully as it can have 'masculinizing' side-effects. Oestrogen patches are sometimes used to treat severe PMS, but progesterone has also to be taken; otherwise there is an increased risk of developing cancer of the uterus. One way of dealing with this is to have an intrauterine system (IUS) fitted. This releases a small amount of progesterone into the uterus.
- **Antidepressants.** Taking a SSRI antidepressant can help to boost serotonin levels and has shown to be effective in treating the psychological symptoms of PMS.
- **Nutritional therapy.** This involves making changes to your diet and possibly taking additional supplements. There is no hard evidence to prove it works, but that doesn't mean that you will not find it effective – anecdotal evidence suggests that nutritional changes help some women. The Natural Health Advisory Service offers telephone consultations and nutritional plans to address the symptoms of PMS (see Useful addresses for contact details). According to the Natural Health Advisory Service, vitamin B, magnesium and zinc are commonly deficient in women with PMS. Studies have been carried out on the use of vitamin B6, agnus castus fruit extract, ginkgo biloba, St John's wort, calcium, magnesium and evening primrose oil. There is some evidence to suggest that calcium and vitamin B6 are effective and preliminary studies indicate that agnus castus, ginkgo

biloba and St John's wort may be useful. There have been conflicting studies on the effectiveness of magnesium and evening primrose oil. There isn't enough evidence yet to say conclusively that any of these supplements are effective for treating PMS.[23]

Before your period it's worth taking extra care with your lifestyle. Practise your relaxation and breathing exercises more often, make more time to unwind. Watch what you eat; many women experience cravings for sweet foods and carbohydrates. Our body's nutritional needs actually increase slightly during this time, which is one explanation for such cravings. So keep an eye on your blood sugar levels because, as we've seen, a drop in blood sugar can trigger a panic attack. Make sure you eat more foods which release energy slowly. You may also need extra snacks.

Pregnancy and birth

This is probably the most life-changing time in a woman's life. At no other time is there so much emotional, physical and hormonal upheaval. For some women, giving birth triggers their anxiety disorder or sparks a setback; for others it is the catalyst that finally gets them over agoraphobia.

Having a baby is a time of huge change for anyone, regardless of whether they have agoraphobia or not. It's a time of joy, happiness and excitement, but it also brings apprehension, tension and worry. Suddenly, you are not only responsible for yourself. You have a beautiful, helpless little being that is totally dependent on you for everything. It's only natural to feel slightly daunted, and it can take a long time to adjust to becoming a mother. Traditionally, a man's role and lifestyle is not affected as much. As a woman, not only will you have gone through many hormonal changes; you will often be the one left at home, during what can seem very long days, caring for your baby.

Sometimes the distraction can be helpful. You can't dwell on your anxieties when there is a baby to feed, change and soothe, clothes to wash and lots of housework to do. But sometimes the tiredness and the sleepless nights can get to you. A baby's cry is designed to cause its mother stress, and a crying baby is certainly not going to help you calm down if you feel panicky or anxious.

Agoraphobia and post-natal depression (PND)

As with PMS, there isn't any clear-cut evidence that says hormonal changes cause post-natal anxiety or depression. But post-natal depression is now a recognized disorder. Even though the term used is 'depression', this type of depressive disorder is known to include a lot of anxiety. So you may experience panic attacks or a panic disorder instead of depression. These feelings may start during pregnancy, rather than after childbirth. If you suffered from agoraphobia before becoming pregnant, tell your GP and midwife – you do have a higher chance of developing post-natal depression. Health professionals are very aware of these conditions nowadays, and you may find it much easier to get help and support than you did before you had a baby.

Hormonal factors

Again, it's useful to understand what is happening to the hormones inside your body. If an egg is fertilized and embeds in the uterus, then the usual drop in oestrogen and progesterone doesn't occur and no period starts. Instead, a new hormone called human chorionic gonadotrophin (HCG) is produced by the developing placenta. It is this hormone which is detected in women's urine by pregnancy tests. After about four months, the placenta takes over from the ovaries and produces its own oestrogen and progesterone. Around the time of birth, other hormones are released which help the womb to contract and after birth, stimulate the production and release of breast milk. After birth, levels of oestrogen and progesterone and other hormones plummet dramatically.

Anecdotal evidence suggests that women with anxiety disorders find their symptoms go away or improve during pregnancy and that they return after giving birth. This suggests that the level of oestrogen plays a part. However, as I've said previously, unfortunately there is no scientific research yet which proves that hormonal changes cause post-natal depression, as no real differences have been found between women with PND and those without it. This could mean that some women are more sensitive to these hormonal changes than others, or that other influences such as social factors play a part.

So, as with PMS, there may be a hormonal link. The same treatment options will be available, such as hormonal therapy or antidepressants. If you are breastfeeding then it's probably not advisable to take antidepressants, but you'll need to weigh up how bad you feel. It may be worth taking them and bottle feeding instead.

Lifestyle factors

Ignoring all the hormonal changes for a moment, there are also many other reasons why you can feel anxious after giving birth and why agoraphobia can be triggered. Adjusting to life with a newborn baby, along with lack of sleep, can be very difficult for all parents. When you have agoraphobia, this is another problem to cope with.

We've already seen that tiredness can be a trigger; now you have a newborn baby, it's often impossible to avoid being tired. You may not eat so well; at first you simply may not have time to cook meals from scratch, and might rely on takeaways and fast foods because it's easier. Finding time to relax can be virtually impossible; lying down to practise your relaxation or breathing exercises will either be interrupted by your baby or you'll just fall asleep. You may have a lot of visitors and simply feel that you don't get a minute to yourself. Having a newborn baby is emotional and physically draining, and if you're prone to panic attacks it's likely you'll experience them at this time.

Getting out and about suddenly becomes a lot more difficult. You can't nip out and get home as quickly as you used to. Suddenly there are prams and car seats to operate, let alone the baby bag packed with bottles, nappies, wipes and everything else you can't go anywhere without. You might find you prefer going out with the baby as you have a pram to hold, and this prop gives you something to hold on to if you feel a bit wobbly. You're also not the centre of attention any more – people will be looking at your baby, not you. But equally, the extra hassle may make it easier for you to stop going out.

Coping with agoraphobia as a mother

Motherhood can be the turning point for women with agoraphobia. If you are the main carer for a baby then you might feel that it isn't acceptable to bring a child up and never leave the house. If you are not housebound, then you may become more aware of your 'boundary' or restrictions. Motherhood represents a good time to tackle your agoraphobia, because you are getting better not just for yourself but for your baby too. This extra motivation can be the push you need to overcome your agoraphobia once and for all.

Take things slowly. It takes time to get used to having a baby and to build a routine. Sleep when your baby sleeps. New mums are often told this, but if you have agoraphobia it's even more important to get as much rest as you need. If there are people around who can help in the early days, do take advantage. Make sure you get as much help as you can from midwives, health visitors and your GP. Health professionals are very aware of post-natal depression and in fact, it can actually seem less of a taboo than to have agoraphobia. You might find it easier and quicker to get support from a counsellor or psychotherapist.

As your baby gets a little older, your day-to-day life should become easier. You should start to get into a routine, your baby should mostly sleep through the night and you will be used to the demands of feeding and changing. Now is the time to really get to grips with your agoraphobia. This would be a good time to start building relaxation and breathing exercises into your day – remember they can be done standing up or as you are walking around. Build some 'me time' into every day, whether this is when your baby has a nap, or a candlelit bath when your partner gets home. If you have eager grandparents, make use of them and make sure you have some time for yourself. You might then be in a position to start tackling situations and start getting out with your baby, using a list like the one described in Chapter 10.

Motherhood is a very rewarding and happy time. Your baby's first smile, first words and first steps are all big milestones. It is hard work and it can be hard to get over agoraphobia as well but it's not impossible. There is no reason why you can't enjoy walks in the park with your baby like other mums. (See Useful addresses for a list of organizations that provide support to mothers.)

Kate
Kate is 32 and overcame her agoraphobia after her daughter was born.

> My agoraphobia was fairly well under control and I was taking antidepressants when I fell pregnant unexpectedly. I had to come off my antidepressants quickly and this was very difficult. I had a few withdrawal effects for the first couple of weeks and also had morning sickness.
>
> The first three months of pregnancy were really difficult. I felt a lot more anxious than I had done for a while and became housebound again. I obviously had to go for regular check-ups at the doctor's and this was a real struggle. I had to go with someone by car.
>
> I was most anxious about walking along by myself and going into large shops. I found it difficult to stand in a queue for a long time and relied on other people getting my shopping for me.
>
> Once I got over the first trimester, I didn't feel so sick and tired. I wasn't working so I was able to have a nap in the afternoon which really helped. I decided that I had to get out a bit, so I tried to go out for a short walk each day. To start off with I just walked around my local area. I lived close to a town centre so I would walk into town and back. I didn't go into any shops at first, I just walked around. It was difficult and I did feel quite dizzy at times. But somehow I managed to get used to this and by the end of my pregnancy I could move around fairly well. I still didn't like

queuing in a busy supermarket but I could go into baby shops and was able to buy everything I needed for the baby.

Immediately after my baby was born, I felt depressed, exhausted and weepy. I was expecting to feel over the moon but I was really tired. I was also quite anaemic, so during the first six weeks I hardly went out at all. Those weeks went by in a blur of feeding the baby, changing nappies, washing dishes and sleeping.

By the time my baby was two months old, she was sleeping through the night. This really helped me get my life together again. I started to find my feet and got into a routine. I was still having panic attacks and my biggest fear was that something would happen to me and I wouldn't be able to look after my baby.

But I started to go out for walks again and holding on to the pram really helped. It was nice to get out and about, I really enjoyed getting out of the house with the baby. I tried to go for a short walk with the baby every day and eventually I found myself going into shops. It was hard navigating my way round shops with a pram but it meant I could focus on the baby and try to ignore any anxious thoughts. I was determined to be a 'normal' mother, I didn't want my baby to be stuck indoors all the time. And it wasn't fair to rely on her dad to take her out when he was working during the day. I knew I had to get better for her.

It's not always been easy and I have had setbacks, but I certainly wouldn't say I'm agoraphobic any more. My daughter is now three and I can go pretty much wherever I want. I drive or walk, we go to playgroups, I can go to the supermarket and do our weekly shop.

I think for me the key was getting out every day. If I'd leave it too long, it would build up into a big deal. Once you're used to going out every day, it eventually gets easier. Before you know it, you're walking out the door without even thinking about panic attacks.

Menopause

The final major hormonal change for women is the menopause. This normally occurs between the ages of 45 and 55. About three to five years before a woman's last period, the function of her ovaries starts to deteriorate. The menstrual cycle may be shorter or longer and periods may become heavier or lighter. Eventually, the level of oestrogen and progesterone produced by the ovaries drops so low that eggs are no longer released and periods stop altogether. When this happens a woman is no longer able to conceive. The menopause can be a time of great physical and psychological change.

Symptoms of the menopause

The following are some of the most common symptoms of the menopause. Like PMS, not every woman will experience symptoms of the menopause and any symptoms will vary in severity:

- hot flushes
- night sweats
- aches and pains
- insomnia
- tiredness
- bladder problems
- panic attacks
- poor memory and concentration
- decrease in sexual desire

It's easy to see how any of these symptoms might trigger an episode of agoraphobia. For someone who has previously suffered from agoraphobia and panic attacks, these changes, like any unusual or sudden physical changes, may easily prompt worrying and alarming thoughts.

Menopause and reducing anxiety

If you are approaching or going through the menopause, this might well be a time to pay extra attention to your relaxation exercises and to practise positive thinking. Even if you have been without agoraphobia for some time, it is worth familiarizing yourself again with strategies to reduce anxious thoughts and tension.

If you do find that the menopause triggers panic attacks and agoraphobia, seek help from your doctor. There are a number of medications you can take, although you need to discuss these and any side-effects with your doctor. Lifestyle changes such as relaxation, and especially changes of diet, can be helpful. You may also need to consider seeing a counsellor or psychotherapist to help you through the episode of agoraphobia and talk through any specific feelings you have about the menopause.

Epilogue

As this book has shown, there are many paths to take which can lead you away from a life at home. There is no magic overnight cure and acceptance will be needed, but a commitment to overcome agoraphobia and perseverance will serve you well on your journey.

Never give up on overcoming agoraphobia, but be aware that, unlike a broken bone, agoraphobia may never truly heal. We all have fears and anxieties. These will never be completely eradicated, nor should they be. They are what make us uniquely human.

You may overcome your agoraphobia and never suffer from it again. Or you may find that a life event triggers the symptoms once more. In that case, go back to basics and work through the strategies you have used successfully in the past.

Arm yourself with as much knowledge as you can about agoraphobia and how anxiety works. This will not only reassure you but will give you the tools to tackle new negative and anxious thoughts. Also, arm yourself with knowledge of CBT techniques and anything else that can help you to change the way you think and behave. If nothing else, this will reinforce the knowledge that your body's reactions are normal and can be overcome.

Make sure you access as many forms of help as you can. Join several charities and take advantage of any self-help groups, telephone courses or helplines that are on offer. Don't shut off the outside world – try to keep as many links to the wider world going as you can.

Ensure you get the support you need from your doctor, whether this is a medication which works for you, psychotherapy or computerized cognitive behavioural therapy. If your doctor shows no understanding of agoraphobia, then change your doctor!

It's easy to feel fed up and think that you'll never get over your agoraphobia. But there are many stories of hope out there and yours could soon be one of them. At the height of my agoraphobia, I was so anxious and agitated that I couldn't physically keep still. I really believed there was something seriously wrong with my body, and that if there wasn't then I must have a serious mental condition. I lived with my mum and there were times when I honestly thought there was no way out. I lost contact with many friends, didn't work and couldn't drive. Just going to the doctor's was a big challenge and I'd return completely exhausted.

If you had told me that I would overcome my fears and go on to write a self-help book about it, I would never have believed you. Now it has been many years since I've suffered from agoraphobia. I can travel wherever I want, including flying abroad. I still feel the beginnings of a panic attack at times, especially if I go out when I'm feeling ill or very tired. But I now know what to say to myself to calm myself down, how to block out the thoughts that will increase my panic.

I've learnt to equip myself with the tools to manage my anxiety and I believe this is something everyone can do. Some of us find it easier than others, some need more support than others, but we can all get there. You simply need to take those first steps and start proving to yourself that your feeling of 'safety' lives inside you and can travel anywhere your body does. Despite how panic attacks make you feel, you do have a choice; you do have control over your life. Recovery is within your power.

References

1. 300.21 'Panic Disorder with Agoraphobia'; 300.22 'Agoraphobia Without History of Panic Disorder' (1994). *DSM-IV: Diagnostic and Statistical Manual of Mental Disorders*, American Psychiatric Association.
2. Ghosh, A. and Marks, I.M. (1987), 'Self-treatment of agoraphobia by exposure', *Behavior Therapy* 18, pp. 3–16.
3. 'Panic attacks and panic disorder', National Phobics Society, March 2004.
4. National Institute for Clinical Excellence (December 2004), 'Anxiety: management of anxiety (panic disorder, with or without agoraphobia and generalized anxiety disorder) in adults in primary, secondary and community care'. NICE Clinical Guideline 22.
5. Hairon, N., 'Survey exposes GP frustration at dire access to depression services', 2 March 2006.
6. Report of CSM working group on the safety of selective serotonin reuptake inhibitor antidepressants, December 2004.
7. NHS Centre for Reviews and Dissemination (2001), *Acupuncture*, Effective Health Care Bulletin 7 (2), p. 12.
8. Fellowes, D., Barnes, K. and Wilkinson, S. (2004), 'Aromatherapy and massage for symptom relief in patients with cancer'. *Cochrane Database of Systematic Reviews* 2004 (2).
9. Tovey, P. (2002), 'A single-blinded trial of reflexology for irritable bowel syndrome'. *British Journal of General Practice* 52, no. 474, pp. 19–23.
10. Kushner, M.G., Sher, K.J. and Beitman, B.D. (1990), 'The relationship between alcohol problems and anxiety disorders'. *American Journal of Psychiatry* 147 (6), pp. 685–95.
11. Deas, D., Gearding, L. and Hazy, J. (2000), 'Marijuana and panic disorder'. *Journal of American Academy of Child & Adolescent Psychiatry* 39 (12), p. 1467; Geracioti, T.D. and Post, R.M. (1991), 'Onset of panic disorder associated with rare use of cocaine'. *Biological Psychiatry* 29 (4), pp. 404–06.
12. Johannsen, A., Asberg, M., Soder, P.O., and Soder, B. (2005), 'Anxiety, gingival inflammation and periodontal disease in non-smokers and smokers – an epidemiological study'. *Journal of Clinical Periodontology* 32 (5), pp. 488–91.
13. Kiecolt-Glaser, J.K., and Glaser, R. (2002), 'Depression and immune function: central pathways to morbidity and mortality'. *Journal of Psychosomatic Research* 53 (4), pp. 873–6.
14. Jacobson, E. (1938), *Progressive Relaxation*, 2nd edn. Chicago: University of Chicago Press.
15. Hazell, J. and Wilkins, A.J. (1990), 'A contribution of fluorescent lighting to agoraphobia'. *Psychological Medicine* 20 (3), pp. 591–6.

111

16. National Institute for Clinical Excellence (December 2004), 'Anxiety: management of anxiety (panic disorder, with or without agoraphobia and generalised anxiety disorder) in adults in primary, secondary and community care'. NICE clinical guideline 22.

17. Andrews, G., Creamer, M., Crino, R. et al (2002), *The Treatment of Anxiety Disorders: Clinician Guides and Patient Manuals.* 2nd edn. Cambridge: Cambridge University Press.

18. Arntz, A. (2003), 'Cognitive therapy versus applied relaxation as treatment of generalized anxiety disorder'. *Behaviour Research and Therapy* 41 (6), pp. 633–46.

19. Press release: 'Johnson announces £170 million boost to mental health therapies', Department of Health, 10 October 2007.

20. National Institute for Health and Clinical Excellence (February 2006), *Computerized cognitive behaviour therapy for depression and anxiety.* Technical Appraisal 97.

21. Vickers, A. and Zollman, C. (1999), 'Clinical review ABC of complementary medicine'. *British Medical Journal* 319, pp. 1346–9.

22. Kirsch, I., Montgomery, G. and Sapirstein, G. (1995), 'Hypnosis as an adjunct to cognitive-behavioral psychotherapy: a meta-analysis'. *Journal of Consultative Clinical Psychology* 63, pp. 214–20.

23. Canning, S., Waterman, M. and Dye, L. (2006), 'Dietary supplements and herbal remedies for premenstrual syndrome (PMS): a systematic research review of the evidence for their efficacy'. *Journal of Reproductive and Infant Psychology* 24 (4), pp. 363–78.

Useful addresses

Charities

First Steps to Freedom
Helpline: 0845 120 2916 (10 a.m.
to 10 p.m. Monday to Thursday; 10
a.m. to midnight Friday to Sunday)
Website: www.first-steps.org

**Mind (National Association for
Mental Health)**
Info Line: 0845 766 0163 (9.15 a.m.
to 5.15 p.m. Monday to Friday)
Website: www.mind.org.uk

National Phobics Society
Zion Community Resource Centre
339 Stretford Road
Hulme
Manchester M15 4ZY
Helpline: 08444 775 774 (9.15 a.m.
to 9 p.m. Monday to Friday)
Website: www.phobics-society.org.
uk

No Panic
Helpline: 0808 808 0545 (10 a.m.
to 10 p.m. every day. From 10 p.m.
to 10 a.m. this telephone number
provides a night-time anxiety crisis
recorded message service.)
Website: www.nopanic.org.uk

Complementary therapies

Acupuncture

**British Medical Acupuncture
Society (BMAS)**
Tel.: 01606 786782
Website: www.medical-acupuncture.
co.uk
Email: admin@medical-acupuncture.
org.uk

Aromatherapy

**International Federation of
Professional Aromatherapists**
Tel.: 01455 637987
Website: www.ifparoma.org
Email: admin@ifparoma.org

Tisserand
Tel.: 01273 325666
Website: www.tisserand.com
Email: info@tisserand.com

Autogenic therapy

The British Autogenic Society
Tel.: 020 7391 8908
Website: www.autogenic-therapy.
org.uk
Email: admin@autogenic-therapy.
org.uk

Bach Flower Remedies

Bach Centre
Tel.: 01491 834678
Website: www.bachcentre.com

Bach Flower Remedies Direct
Tel.: 020 8773 3803
Website: www.bachshop.co.uk

Buteyko Breathing Method

Buteyko Breathing Association
Tel.: 01277 366906
Website: www.buteykobreathing.org

Herbal medicine

**National Institute of Medical
Herbalists**
Tel.: 01392 426022
Website: www.nimh.org.uk
Email: nimh@ukexeter.freeserve.
co.uk

Homeopathy

Society of Homeopaths
Tel.: 0845 450 6611
Website: www.homeopathy-soh.org
Email: info@Homeopathy-Soh.Org

Reflexology

Association of Reflexologists
Tel.: 0870 5673320
Website: www.aor.org.uk
Email: info@aor.org.uk

Dental supplies

Boots.com
Tel.: 08456 090 055
Website: www.boots.com

Distance learning

Open University
Telephone: 0845 300 60 90
Website: www.open.ac.uk

Learn Direct
Telephone: 08000 150 450 from
7a.m. to 11p.m. 7 days a week
Website: www.learndirect.co.uk

Exercise

GAIAM Direct
Tel.: 0870 241 5471
Website: www.gaiamdirect.co.uk
Email: sales@gaiamdirect.co.uk

Health services

BUPA
Tel.: 0800 600 500
Website: www.bupa.co.uk

NHS Direct
Tel.: 0845 4647 (24 hours)

Helpline and search facility for
local health services (GPs, dentists,
opticians and pharmacies).

Lifestyle

Alcohol and substance dependency

Alcoholics Anonymous
Tel.: 0845 769 7555 (24 hours a day
every day)
Website: www.alcoholics-
anonymous.org.uk

FRANK
Helpline: 0800 77 66 00 (24 hours a
day every day, for problems related
to drugs)
Website: www.talktofrank.com
Email: frank@talktofrank.com

Nutrition

**British Association for Applied
Nutrition and Nutritional Therapy**
Tel.: 08706 061284
Website: www.bant.org.uk
Email: theadministrator@bant.org.
uk

**The Food and Mood Community
Interest Company**
Website: www.foodandmood.org
Email: websiteinfo@foodandmood.
org

Holland & Barrett
Tel.: 0870 606 6605 (for ordering,
8.30 a.m. to 8 p.m. weekdays; 9
a.m. to 5 p.m. Saturdays)
Website: www.hollandandbarrett.
com
Email: hbcustsrv@
hollandandbarrett.com

Smoking cessation

NHS Stop Smoking Service
Helpline: 0800 169 0 169 (7 a.m. to
11 p.m. every day)
Website: http://gosmokefree.nhs.uk

Psychological therapies

Computerized cognitive behaviour therapy

FearFighter
Tel.: 0121 233 2873
Website: www.fearfighter.com
Email: enquiries@fearfighter.com

The following entries in this section cover therapist member organizations, directories of relevant therapists and/or search facilities:

British Association for Behavioural and Cognitive Psychotherapies
Tel.: 0161 797 4484
Website: www.babcp.com

National Register of Hypnotherapists and Psychotherapists
National Enquiry Line: 01282 716839
Website: http://www.nrhp.co.uk
Email: admin@nrhp.co.uk

United Kingdom Council for Psychotherapy
Tel.: 020 7014 9955
Website: www.psychotherapy.org.uk

Relaxation training

Meditainment
Tel.: 01273 325136 (for ordering)
Website: www.meditainment.com

Seasonal Affective Disorder

The Seasonal Affective Disorder Association
Website: www.sada.org.uk

BriteBox
Tel.: 0800 1388 567 (8 a.m. to 9 p.m. every day)
Website: www.britebox.co.uk
Email: info@goldstaff.net

Women's health

Meet-a-Mum Association
Telephone: 0845 120 3746
(Weekdays 7 p.m. to 10 p.m.)
Website: www.mama.co.uk

National Childbirth Trust
Pregnancy and Birth Line: 0870 444 8709 10 a.m. to 8 p.m., Monday to Friday
Website: www.nct.org.uk

Natural Health Advisory Service
Tel.: 01273 609699
Website: www.naturalhealthas.com
Email: enquiries@naturalhealthas.com

Work and state benefits

Benefit Enquiry Line
Tel.: 0800 88 22 00

Citizens' Advice Bureau
Website: www.citizensadvice.org.uk

Employment Tribunals Service
Public Enquiry Line: 0845 795 9775
Website: www.employmenttribunals.gov.uk

Equality and Human Rights Commission
Helpline (England): 0845 604 6610
Helpline (Scotland): 0845 604 5510
Helpline (Wales): 0845 604 8810
Website: www.equalityhumanrights.com
Email: info@equalityhumanrights.com

Further reading

As explained in this book, bibliotherapy can be of real help, especially if you're housebound – books are even prescribed by some doctors.

All books are available from Amazon.co.uk or through bookshops unless alternative ordering details are given.

Bourne, Edmund J., *The Anxiety & Phobia Workbook*. New Harbinger, Oakland, CA, revd edn 2005.

Butler, Gillian, *Overcoming Social Anxiety and Shyness*. Robinson, London, 1999.

Butler, G. and Hope, T., *Manage Your Mind*. Oxford University Press, Oxford, 1995. Order from <www.oup.co.uk>, call 01536 741727 or email bookorders.uk@oup.com

Davis, M. et al, *The Relaxation and Stress Reduction Workbook*. New Harbinger, Oakland, CA, 2000.

Gallop, Rick, *The GI Diet*. Virgin Publishing, London, 2005.

Ingham, Christine, *Panic Attacks*. HarperCollins, London, 1997.

Kennerley, Helen, *Overcoming Anxiety*. Robinson, London, 1997. See also the website <www.overcoming.co.uk>.

Marks, Professor I. M., *Living With Fear*. McGraw-Hill Education, Columbus, OH, 2005.

Rowe, Dorothy, *Beyond Fear*. HarperCollins, London, 2002.

Silove, D. and Manicavasagar, V., *Overcoming Panic*. Robinson, London, 1997.

Stewart, Maryon, *Cruising Through the Menopause*. Vermilion, London, 2000.

Stewart, M. et al, *No More PMS*. Vermilion, London, 1997.

Weekes, Dr Claire, *Essential Help for Your Nerves*. Thorsons, London, 2000. Other titles by her include *Self Help for Your Nerves* (Thorsons, 1995) and *Simple Effective Treatment of Agoraphobia* (currently out of print in the UK, but may be available secondhand via Amazon or through libraries). She has also produced an audio tape: *Moving to Freedom – Going on Holiday*, which is available from <www.drclaireweekes.co.uk> .

Williams, Chris, *Overcoming Anxiety: A Five Areas Approach*. Hodder Arnold, London, 2003.

The Oxford Cognitive Therapy Centre publishes a number of self-help booklets about overcoming anxiety, including:

Managing Anxiety (Gillian Butler – also available in Punjabi, Hindi, Gujarati and Urdu);
Overcoming Social Anxiety (Gillian Butler);
Controlling Anxiety (Melanie Fennell and Gillian Butler);
Building Self-Esteem (Helen Jenkins and Melanie Fennell);

Managing Anxiety: A User's Manual (Helen Kennerley);
Understanding Health Anxiety (Christine Kuchemann and Diana Sanders);
Overcoming Phobias (Diana Sanders);
Understanding Panic (David Westbrook and Khadija Rouf).

The Centre also stocks a relaxation tape and instruction sheet: *How to Relax* (Rachel Norris and Christine Kuchemann).
Call 01865 223986 or visit <www.octc.co.uk> to order.

Index